The Stories of 210
Faithful People

Pathways to Faith

Gordon E. Jackson with
Phyllisee Foust Jackson

Abingdon Press
Nashville

Pathways to Faith: The Stories of 210 Faithful People

Copyright © 1989 by Abingdon Press

All rights reserved.
No part of this work may be reproduced or transmitted in any form or by any means, electronic or mechanical, including photocopying and recording, or by any information storage or retrieval system, except as may be expressly permitted by the 1976 Copyright Act or in writing from the publisher. Requests for permission should be addressed in writing to Abingdon Press, 201 Eighth Avenue South, Nashville, TN 37202.

This book is printed on acid-free paper.

Library of Congress Cataloging-in-Publication Data

Jackson, Gordon E., 1918-
   Pathways to faith : the stories of 210 faithful people / Gordon E. Jackson and Phyllisee Foust Jackson.
    p. cm.
   ISBN 0-687-30351-6 (pbk. : alk. paper)
   1. Faith (Theology) 2. Protestants—United States.
3. Christianity—Psychology. I. Jackson, Phyllisee Foust.
II. Title.
BT771.2.J33 1989
248.2—dc19
                                          88-22215
                                               CIP

ISBN 0-687-30351-6

Scripture quotations are from the Revised Standard Version of the Bible, copyright 1946, 1952, 1971 by the Division of Christian Education of the National Council of Churches of Christ in the USA. Used by permission.

Manufactured by the Parthenon Press at
Nashville, Tennessee, United States of America

Pathways to Faith

To our parents,
in grateful memory

Contents

- Introduction.. 9
1. Stages Along the Way: Three Forms of Faith...19
2. Human Needs: Clamorings for Faith.............. 49
3. The Return to Roots..65
4. Communal Encounters: Feeders of Faith in Adult Years.. 90
5. The Bible: Almost Closed............................ 111
6. Prayer: Number Two But Narrow.................128
7. The Sacraments: What's Wrong?.................. 142
8. The Sermon: An Impossible Task?................155
9. Faith Facing the World: The Ethical Dimension.. 168
10. Some Final Gleanings................................. 180

Introduction

This study is a limited attempt to find out empirically how faith is formed. For twenty years part of my teaching assignment at Pittsburgh Theological Seminary was in the area of spiritual formation. We read many of the spiritual classics, but I kept wondering how more typical men and women might tell the story of their faith.

It occurred to me that we should ask some faithful women and men to reflect on how their faith came to be. Then out of their spiritual autobiographies we might be able to develop themes that might be helpful to the fundamental task of the church: the forming of faith. And yet, I asked myself, is not that the very question with which the writers of the devotional classics wrestled? It is the question in the profound sense that the classics have come out of experience with God within the context of daily living. This is the only crucible in which faith is formed. But there seemed to me to be three profound distinctions between those giants whose works have become classics and most of the rest of us. We are all disciples together, but many of them were religious geniuses, meaning that their discipleship took a wonderful but peculiar turn in terms of intensity, sensitivity, and insightfulness. Furthermore, many of them were cloistered, their lives devoted in atypical ways to the things of the Spirit. At least their adult home life was vastly different, as they lived out their lives in sisterhoods and brotherhoods and in celibacy. Finally, their vocations were basically religious, that is, lived, thought, and written about in that dimension, while the more typical faithful woman or man functions mainly in a secular dimension. She or he must move from the daily work pattern into the world of Bible, prayer, meditation, and worship. Might that move itself make a vast difference in how faith is formed?

Then came the question, Where would modern Protestant clergy fit? In the dimension of the religious? In the secular dimension? They, too, should be asked to tell the story of their faith journeys.

While I was searching for a way to conduct this study, my wife, Phyllisee, was working on her doctoral dissertation, for which she was doing in-depth interviewing and factor analysis. Her methodology seemed appropriate to my concerns. It would involve an in-depth interview, as non-directed and open-ended as possible, a careful analysis of the taped interview, and a patient allowing of the data gathered from the several interviews to form themes about the growing of faith.

Several advanced students, Phyllisee, and I developed a pilot project. Over a two-year period the students, following a training program, interviewed scores of women and men to elicit from them their stories of how their faith had come to be. As a result of the pilot project we determined (1) to limit our study to people from thirty-five to fifty-five years of age, allowing for both the accumulation of lived experience and time for reflection to mature; (2) to use only two interviewers, Phyllisee and myself, the better to control variables in the interviewing process; and (3) to limit our study to the six mainline Protestant denominations in which approximately half

Introduction

of all Protestants find their church homes. We were painfully aware that this limitation would sacrifice important data from the Roman Catholic, Orthodox Catholic, and Episcopal traditions, as well as important sect-type communions. Finally, we determined we must include both professionals in religion (e.g., pastors and seminary professors) and laypeople.

We interviewed 150 laypeople (75 women and 75 men) and 60 professionals,* (36 pastors and 24 seminary professors), including both men and women. The 210 people represented United Methodists, Presbyterians, American Baptists, Southern Baptists, Lutherans (American Lutheran Church and Lutheran Church in America), and United Church of Christ. They lived in the Northeast, Southeast, Midwest, Northwest, and Southwest of the United States. We had wondered if there might be regional differences, and we found none of significance.

The pastors and seminary professors were suggested by peers and colleagues across the country. The laypeople were selected by their pastors, most of whom we did not know. We called the pastors, explained our research study, and asked if they would choose from their congregations a woman and a man, between thirty-five and fifty-five whom they regarded as persons exemplifying faith. We did not define faith, but we did suggest that it did not necessarily point to the most institutionally active people. Then we wrote or called these people to see if they would help us in our study of how faith is formed by letting us interview them. We told them the interviews would be taped, but we promised them confidentiality. Arrangements were made to see them wherever it was most convenient for them: home, church, office, and in one instance, a park bench.

---

*Throughout the book the term "professional" is limited to those whose profession is in the field of religion, that is, pastors and professors.

The study sought the spiritual autobiographies, to borrow from Simone Weil, of 210 people. The interviews did not proceed along a set of preestablished questions. Each was told, "I am trying to find out how faith is formed. Will you tell me, starting wherever you will, how your faith has come to be? I'll simply listen and perhaps enter with a question here and there for clarification." The interviews, all taped, lasted from one to two and a half hours. The interview material was listened to by the authors, the data carefully factored, and themes gradually began to emerge. The rich data of the interviews have provided the empirical material for this book. Some wonderfully faithful people have shared with us their spiritual odysseys. We have tried to be faithful to their stories.

The amazing diversity by which people come to faith was expressed poetically by Rabbi Nahman of Bratislava: "God chooses one man with a shout, another with a song, another with a whisper."[1] The people we interviewed spelled out a rich diversity, some in patterned ways as though they were walking along well-beaten paths, others in idiosyncratic ways as though they were making new forays parallel to, or around, the established paths. There were charismatics whose emotional histories seemed to demand a more affective expression of what was churning inside of them. The pilgrimage belonged to each, with a lot of similarities but no sameness.

There was the self-defined conservative who saw the urgent need for liberals because in his experience too many conservatives became paralyzed when it comes to action. There were liberals who acknowledged that the fires that were driving them were kindled by fundamentalist parents and grandparents. There was one man whose nominal faith became vibrant as he captained stewardship drives and kept goading others about their responsibility. That goading had had a reverse action within him. Money had been his god until he had to account for his money before God. And there were those who found faith through the traditional means of grace, that is, the Eucharist, prayer, and the Bible. For a few, the arts fertilized their faith. Nature played a role for many, as eyes of faith followed its pointing finger to the magnitude of God the Creator. *How* each individual made his or her pilgrimage of faith, and out of what stuff, determined largely *what* his or her faith was all about.

Most of their experiences were written into their faith consciousness through an evolutionary process, but for a few faith consciousness became crystallized through a revolutionary conversion experience. However, for the 10 percent who had a radical turnaround in their faith journeys, the total faith story was no more compelling than was the story of the other 90 percent. For neither the 10 percent nor the 90 percent was there faith without wrenching. Pain there was; but there was also deep satisfaction, for they sensed that they were on a growth journey. The pain for some was divesting the self of old images, treadmill fixations, and neurotic anxieties, often through psychotherapy, until parents and other significant people whom they had interiorized and by whom they had defined themselves began to emerge as distinct from themselves. Gradually God, too, began to emerge as distinct from "Dad" or "Mom" or some other close person. Especially did the person in therapy have to get rid of old hang-ups about God being critically watchful, vengeful, and manipulative, and replace these images with those of a loving and freeing parent. Then faith could take a small step for some, or what seemed like a quantum leap to others, on its journey. The pain for many was more like growing pains, the aches of changing, redirecting, reorienting, rethinking, renewing. It was the wrenching of maturing, of leaving comfortable levels where they had felt somewhat at home to proceed like Abraham toward a new life. Not one used the word "adventure," but that is what their stories sounded like. Perhaps none would have dared to think of himself or herself as a miniature Abraham, but each seemed to be questing through terrain that was new and exciting, though sometimes scary for them.

As we listened to these life stories, repeatedly there came to mind Ludwig Binswanger's "inner biography" and Alfred Schutz's "lived experience." Both terms suggest a unity of content within each person, made up of personal experiencing of the world, including the responses each makes to the stuff of life. There was rich duration of content within each of them. Faith is one way they responded to the myriad givens that constituted their inner biographies that composed their lived experience. Within the biographies of each, only a fragment of which could they share with us, was an accumulation of thirty-five to fifty-five years of experiencing, of living through, atomistic bits of working, loving, hating, sleeping, fearing, embracing, pulling back, going forward, feeling, thinking, intending, listening, seeing, worshiping, and more. They were a seamless web of experiencing. Within the milieu of all their experiencing, faith was occurring, taking hold, pointing. It was very hard for most to say, "That was the critical moment; that's when it happened." An isolated experience was rarely lifted up. Even when it was, it was not dwelt upon as all-encompassing, all-important, all-consuming. It was like a light illuminating the roadway but requiring other lights up ahead. Religious experiences, spiritual high points, and peak experiences were serendipitous occasions helping them to bring into focus God and the rest of their experiences. These brief general reflections may provide a flavor to our study.

The more detailed results we have tried to present in this book. We who have had the privilege of listening into the lives of 210 fellow travelers acknowledge that the

Introduction

pages of a book cannot do justice to the riches they shared with us. But we have tried to be faithful reporters and to outline appropriate implications where they might be saying something significant to the churches about their major task: the forming of faith. Our reporting differs from that of Professor James Fowler, who has drawn correlations with psychological material, especially that of Erik Erikson.[2] The interest motivating our study was not interdisciplinary, as valuable as that is, but ecclesial: what might the church learn from the faith stories of faithful people?

We have tried to guard against the easy generalization. Indeed, we have sought not to generalize from our data. Nor has our interest been to cite a lot of figures and to supply graphs and charts (although we have had to develop statistical analyses to enable us to find pointers along the way). Rather, we have sought to present the storied data and let those data say what they might to assist in the growing of faith. At many points, however, we have tried to interpret the data and make concrete proposals toward resolving some of the problems our interviewees surfaced for us. While we have not been bashful about making suggestions that might enrich the faith journeys cited, we have not intended to make this book a compendium of resource materials. Yet along the way we have cited resources, even leaning on some of them, that we think could inform the churches' efforts to help faith take hold and grow.

We think there needs to be a great deal more empirical research into how faith is formed. Our study, along with Fowler's and others, is but a beginning. Other studies are needed to explore the forming of faith within the Catholic tradition, black churches, and the sects. A focus on other ages—twenty-five to thirty-five and post-sixty—should make for rich and important studies. A tantalizing study would be of brothers and sisters of faithful women and men who are agnostic, atheistic, or who have simply rejected the church. There were at least twenty of these siblings among our interviewees. What contributed to these differences between brothers and sisters in relatively the same household might be exceedingly informative.

While we are not generalizing from this small study, there is a general formula for the forming of faith that we believe emerges from our sample. It would go something like this: get born into a conservative home, one with acceptance and understanding, and with integrity but not much in the way of worldly goods. Grow up in a small church that becomes an extended family. Meet a few significant people along the way, especially in adolescence and young and middle adulthood. Have some broadening experiences, often traumatic ones, upon which you do some hard reflecting. Fueled perhaps by religious fires lighted in childhood and/or adolescence, interpret your experience by a constantly growing belief system, the roots of which are in a perduring trust and a vision that risks commitment. Find ways to express your faith by getting involved, and keep yourself open to the Numinous Reality always addressing you.

Nearly every introduction closes with some expression of gratitude. So does this one, because the pages themselves would cry out if we failed this expression. We met some superb human beings who shared with us strangers the innermost stories of their beings: how they came to faith, as far as they were consciously aware. Their sharings included, of course, non-faith development, which helped form the framework for their faith. Our efforts to capture what they shared pale beside what they gave to us. Phyllisee and I have been given gifts: the life stories of housewives, farmers, teachers, lawyers, preachers, dry cleaners, engineers, car salesmen, and

Introduction

realtors, to name but a few. Codification is necessary, but codification is bland compared to the richness of the living documents. Autobiographies shared with us have informed our beings. Our hope is that our retelling by way of this report is neither unfaithful nor too distilled nor too bland. Throughout, we have tried to protect their identities.

The interviews furnished us with so much material that a friend, Dr. Floyd H. Taylor, Research Professor of Community Medicine (along with Bruce Barnhill, his research associate), of the School of Medicine of the University of Pittsburgh, put the data into computers. We are grateful to them for this generous and valuable contribution. Our thanks to Evelyn Rehse for seeing the manuscript through revision upon revision, in her gracious and meticulous way, is almost unmeasurable.

We are also grateful to the students who contributed so much to this study and whose encouragement lies back of this book. Not only did they learn the art of interviewing and the skill of factoring their data; they also reflected much on what they heard, and their reflections have contributed to this book.

We are appreciative of the many clergy and lay groups with whom we have shared some vignettes and insights out of our study. Their probing questions, their encouragement, and their expectations have been energetic prodders to us to get on with the writing.

Although much of the study was self-financed, it would not have been possible had it not been for a generous fellowship grant from the Association of Theological Schools, which underwrote a sabbatical. Mrs. Lenore Clark Joseph generously made a gift to the research fund in memory of her husband, Parker Clark. Our hope is that this study fulfills at least some of the expectations of their invested trust.

Now I have a debt I have longed to pay in public. It is to

Phyllisee, my wife, who provided the model for this research, who did a third of the interviewing and all of the factoring of the material, who shared her observations and insights with me and balanced many of mine, and who entered into my writing now and then by asking in her gentle way, "Do you really think that's what they said?" or, "Do you really want to say it that way?" Thanks, Phyl, for the team effort.

Gordon E. Jackson

NOTES

1. Quoted by Lawrence LeShan, *How to Meditate* (Boston: Little, Brown, 1974), p. 45.
2. Professor James W. Fowler is also engaged in research in faith formation. See his *Stages of Faith* (San Francisco: Harper & Row, 1981).

CHAPTER • 1

*Stages Along the Way:
Three Forms of Faith*

As we began our interviews, many asked, "What do you mean by faith?" We replied that we did not want to try to define faith, since we were interested in the process by which they had come to faith. Therefore however they thought of faith, what did that journey entail? What we discovered is that faith is a most ambiguous word. The subjects in our study, especially the professionals,* seemed to differentiate faith into three basic forms: trust, commitment, and belief. Sometimes one form would emerge into prominence, sometimes another. Out of the 210 interviews we were able to distill the structure of each form and locate the three forms in relation to each other.

Faith as Trust

The people in our study seemed to experience both a generalized trust and a focused trust. The latter has as its primary object God. The former is more generic.

---

*Most of the quotations in this chapter come from the professionals, who had reflected more deeply on the meaning of faith and who articulated those reflections more clearly. But the quoted material reflects lay experience at the trust and commitment levels, though not at the belief level, for reasons cited in that section.

H. Richard Niebuhr has aptly described this more generalized trust as follows: "Faith is the attitude of the self in its existence toward all the existences that surround it, as being to be relied upon or to be suspected. It is the attitude that appears in all the wariness and confidence of life as it moves about among the living. It is fundamentally trust or distrust in being itself."[1]

Faith as trust is an attitudinal response to the material of life. The objects of this trust are manifold, the quality varied, but the trust itself is a response common to the human condition. Our interviewees were witnesses to trust as a basic response to all that fed their lives. A professor of drama talked about this form of faith in these words: "Every time I direct a play, faith is involved—faith in each student, in the cast, faith in them as they get up there, faith in God, too, for I'm sort of praying them through."

Most of the people described their trust as it focused on God in religious terms. A businessman talked about his faith as "nonintellectual; at least that's the bottom line, where it's most basic for me. I just have a profound, personal sense about God: that God is uniquely related to the person of Jesus. That's what I trust; that's my basic faith."

Trust as Perduring Assurance

The men and women in our study had suffered and enjoyed, lost and won, doubted and believed, regressed and progressed through their faith journey. But in none was there despair; in all there was hope. With almost all, doubt was a periodic visitor or a constant companion, as we shall see later in this chapter, but doubt seemed always to be presupposing trust, not looking for it. While it is an interpretative move on our part, we sensed a primitive trust formation in most of them. They seemed to evidence a substratum of feeling tones, which formed an enduring pattern, that things are all right "out there" and all right "in here," meaning within the person. The home and to some degree the church seemed to provide a pervasive sense that things were basically right, and this sense appears to have been a strong part of their inheritance.

We have some direct testimony to this early trust formation. One pastor said, "Mother helped with formation of trust, while from Father I got the strength to go into an adverse situation and stay with what I believe." Another pastor said simply, "Basic trust I grew up with." Many laypeople and professionals used this language: "I can't remember when I didn't have faith." One described trust as an "unconditional stroke without merit, a sense of being loved for my own sake. In that sense it [trust] has the same meaning with reference to God as it did toward my father and mother back there." Said another, "At the root of my life is the conviction that God is trustworthy, and I trust in his trustworthiness. That's enough for life and death." A number of laypeople asked an identical question, as though of themselves: is this sort of faith instinctive? A dentist said, "It seems a constitutional part of myself. It feels like predestination might feel if it were a feeling. I wonder if my faith is planted in me and overlaid with postnatal experiences?"

One professor put the whole matter of trust so richly that we are quoting him at length:

"Faith has been the quiet assumption through the course of my life. I have the quiet confidence that there is in the background, behind the immediate dilemmas, a support, a presence, a force and plan. Behind the appearances is the steady hand of God. I learned from the bosom of my family this kind of trust: that whatever

God does with you is best for you. Faith is dependence on experience: trust in family and the people I love. It is perduratively there. That perduring surety is liberating. No matter what happens to you, you are in God's hands. That force is not hostile. Life is centered at a very elemental level on a kind of goodness.

"My perduring assurance allows me to escape from calculations. Freedom came when I realized I didn't have to exercise my mind or heart or energies to calculate my future. I could get on with the present. That freedom began to allow me to do one thing: will God's intentions. That did not come originally through rational antennae. Somehow it grew up inside me. When it got articulated, helped by such giants as Augustine, Calvin, Wesley, Frances, it made sense, but it was an articulation of something I knew well within myself. And freedom based on trust has liberated me for creativity; out of security born of trust, creative work has occurred.

"I'm not that worried about the frustrations and distractions anymore. I have tenure in the profound sense that my whole life is tenured. Out of the security of that tenure comes the active mode, that is, the creative mode. Part of my joy lies in this creative mode liberated by trust."

The "perduring assurance" that gives "tenure" to life is what they meant by trust. It was represented in two types of experience.

One type, by far the majority, represents early rootage and growth through struggle. A professor, after reflecting in our presence on Romans 4 and the Abrahamic experience of faith, said, "Trust is pretty basic for me: faith, confidence, trust in this tremendous God." His trust came initially from a fundamentalist home and had been painfully redirected in graduate school in Europe, where he agonized about losing his faith, so radically were his beliefs being reformulated.

Representing a deviation within this type was an interviewee whose home did not provide a basis for trust but whose early church experience did. He remembered always searching for a way for human beings to live together without fighting. Therefore, what was said in Sunday school about forgiveness had central meaning for him. Through Sunday school he began to put his trust in "some ultimate source of forgiveness." It was after graduate school that he came to a crisis in his belief. Through that crisis he learned that faith is at least an "unformed trust in God, and in this form it is deeper than any understanding one has of God premised on that faith." During this intense struggle he identified with Bellow's *Herzog* who cried, "Thou movest me." There was Another in whose hands he was, who would not abandon him. This man began his interview with "Faith is wholehearted trust in the God of the Gospels."

The second type, much in the minority but equally splendid in trust, is illustrated by those who had a dramatic religious experience, the certainty and power of which have remained with them. Though the experiences are different, the point of trust is the same. We visit the conversion experience one of our interviewees had in late adolescence in the privacy of his own room. The words of Jesus came to him: "Him who comes to me I will in no wise cast out." In commenting on his experience, he said, "At bottom is a commitment since seventeen. The universe at the fundamental level is friendly and good. That derives from the initial conception: if I came to Christ, messed up as I was, he would accept me." For him there was a dramatic experience on the basis of which he settled in, gaining a kind of body knowledge that what Jesus Christ represents is trustworthy.

Another illustration of this second type is the woman whose childhood home filled her with self-hate, hatred of her mother, and ambivalence toward her father whom she adored but hated for his weakness. At twenty-three she was hospitalized for a breakdown and at twenty-three she married. She was in therapy off and on from age fifteen to twenty-three. At twenty-six she began to trust God. Here are her words: "As in my therapy group so with God: I fell back and trusted, and God was there. My husband proved himself as trustworthy. He completely accepted me as I was. His acceptance of me was my clue to Christ: that must be the way he accepts me. So about twenty-six I gave up, let God in, and found God to be thoroughly trustworthy. Then my life began to change. I got the sense that Jesus loves me. That was my doorway to trust. Now I step out in a lot of trust, trusting that God is going to be there. Is positiveness another word for trust?" she asked. "That's what trust means to me. God doesn't throw anything away. So I can trust him."

An engineer played his trust off against doubt. "My doubts have terrified me. But two or three times I was sure God had touched me in a personal way, generally after prayer. On those occasions I was flooded with joy. It's so contrary to my nature and to my work as an engineer, but I just knew God was going to take care of my life. I can look back on those times when he touched me and I began to handle my doubts. In that trust, doubt and the turmoil it brings seems to me to promote growth . . . but it is so difficult."

Whether trust gathers out of a more inchoate multiplicity of early experience and is refined and sharpened through struggle, as in type one, or whether it focuses on a dramatic moment of time, as in type two, it would seem to be a fairly primitive, strongly somatic, foundational form of faith, whether it happens in childhood or adulthood.

Paradigms of Trust

We are suggesting two paradigms of trust, one from psychology and the other from the Bible, to picture the basic response to which our witnesses pointed.

The psychological paradigm describes the first year of life, with its psycho-social development described and labeled by Erik H. Erikson as Basic Trust versus Mistrust.[2] The constant "world" of the infant is the mother or "mothering figure." The mother is incorporated into the infant through a quite physical act, the feeding process, in which the baby "takes in" not only the mother's milk but also her odors, her warmth, the rhythmic movements of her breathing, the "feel" of her arms and hands, the sound of her voice, and her attitudes and feelings. Through the process of incorporation, the mother becomes lodged within the infant. Erikson has shown through his studies that the infant comes out of the first year of life with basic trust or mistrust derived from the mothering figure. Basic trust is an attitude blending into the total personality. Trust so formed is a bodily feeling about oneself and one's world. It is a somatic response of well-being, made along the way to the feeders of one's life, and gradually generalized into a habit of the soul.

This paradigm of infant trust is valuable for several reasons. It describes the deepest level of human development, the oral stage, which is the foundation upon which the other forms of faith are built. It shows how all identifications are made out of the stuff of life "out there" that is introjected and made part of the me "in here." It demonstrates the significance of the feeders of life, early ones as well as later, who feed their lives into the stream of each life. The infant develops the most elementary reliance as he or she relies on the reliability of others, and the most rudimentary trust as he or she learns to trust the trustworthiness of others. From Erikson we have learned that beginning with the very first year of life, trust is axial to human existence. The forming of trust does not cease, of course, with infancy. Our people found that their trust deepened and broadened as other nurturing people moved into their adolescent and adult lives, contributing to a somatic sense of continuing well-being. Their own unconscious and conscious experiences of God, momentary as they might be, became the final ground of ultimate trust.

Trust has a much longer religious than psychological history. It is a biblical and theological word referring to profound religious experience. The transition from a more generalized sense of trusting, as discussed by Erikson, to a more specialized sense, as dealt with in religion, is made easy for us to understand by Robert McAfee Brown in his book *Is Faith Obsolete?*[3] Brown, who does not isolate the trust form of faith, points us to Père Olivier Rabut, O.P., who suggests that the root *mn*, which in Hebrew gives us the words "faith" and "belief," has the primitive meaning "to carry a suckling child." As Rabut himself says, "This implies a benevolent care on the part of the supporter and a confident dependence on the part of him who is supported.... Faith consists in relying upon the strength of an Other because this Other is solid."[4] He translates II Chronicles 20:20 as "Rest on the strength of Jahve and you will be fortified." The connections with Erikson's notion of trust are patent, first through the direct reference to the "suckling child" and second through the words "confident dependence," "relying," and "rest," which get at the heart of trust formation.

The notion of trust is in both the Old and New Testaments. Artur Weiser says that in the Prophets and especially in Deutero-Isaiah there is a certainty in God that is at the deepest levels of human existence,

Stages Along the Way: Three Forms of Faith

a certainty that can deal with the threats of human existence.[5] This certainty is deeper than intellectual conviction and bears the pervasive sense of trust. Alan Richardson makes the point that in the New Testament trust is confident reliance upon God's faithfulness.[6] It is so used by Paul in Romans 4:17-20, where Abraham's confidence in God's power is to the fore and so he can trust implicitly in the fulfilment of the divine promise. In fact, Paul's paradigm for this trusting response is Abraham. Romans 4 is Paul's commentary on Genesis 15:6. God had promised Abraham an heir, but at one hundred years of age he was as good as dead, as was Sarah. Yet God reaffirmed the promise. The Genesis story says simply, "And he believed the Lord." Paul is using Abraham as his model for justifying faith. He wrote to the Romans that Abraham was "fully convinced that God was able to do what he had promised" (Rom. 4:21). In his commentary on Romans, C. H. Dodd says, "Abraham relied simply and completely on the all-sufficient power of God." And he goes on to say that what is important in the Pauline passage before us is that faith is "an original and permanent element of all genuinely religious life."[7] We are taking faith in the form of trust to be this original and permanent element: complete reliance on God. An engineer said it this way: "Faith is trust that lets you venture, even fall on your face, and start again; trusting is the adventure." It is trust in the deep visceral sense of bottoming down into this God. We are seeing that this reliance in the religious domain is informed by that more generalized attitude of trust so well described by H. Richard Niebuhr and nailed down in the very first year of life by Erik Erikson. We think that the subjects of our study exemplify and affirm such basic trust.

From our study it would seem that trust has a quasi-instinctual character to it, about which a number of people wondered out loud. This gives it its primal dimension in the structure of faith. Trust and mistrust are fundamental ways of relating to the feeders of one's life, and this relating begins early and runs deep. But whenever it begins and however much it grows, trust is an experience of childhood, a settling down into the feeders and the ultimate Feeder of our lives. It is a set of basic, primitive feeling tones that are fundamentally more bodily and visceral than cognitive. It stamps one's being and colors a whole way of looking at the world. Our study is certainly atypical in that trust became, early on or later, a formative response of everyone in the group. We think this suggests that trust as a visceral response is crucial to faith formation, which points up what is equally crucial: a trustworthy world in which to trust!

Faith as Commitment

Commitment is one theme upon which unanimity pervaded the group, although their descriptions of commitment have the richness of idiosyncratic thrust and flavor. In brief, our people said that commitment is at the core of faith. It is that form of faith which points the self in a life-engrossing direction. That direction helps to stamp indelibly who one is.

Commitment seems to stand as a middle term between trust and belief. If trust is a relational word depicting a bottoming down into the providers of life, and if belief is a propositional word articulating meaning, commitment takes part of its strength from trust as it lives toward and with the trusted objects, and it informs belief as it is out ahead of belief at the frontiers of spirit.

Our people tended to use commitment as a directional word suggesting the pitch of one's life, the deepest underlying intention of the self. It is a picture of the self standing on tiptoe and pitched forward toward the actualizing of a lifelong "project." The Hebrew word for "soul," *nephesh*, carries this meaning of directionality: the soul directed toward God. Martin Buber has emphasized "intention of faith" in this sense of directionality, describing it as the "innermost action of man."[8] Our study found 210 people with this "intention," their lives pitched in the direction of God in whom they had deposited trust and about whom at least some were reflecting.

The Role of the Will

While it would be an obvious error to assign commitment to willing, as though feeling and thinking were foreign to its experience, will played a decisive role in the faith formation of these people. As we listened to the several ways in which they recounted their commitment, we were reminded again and again of Josiah Royce and William James. Royce, in *The Philosophy of Loyalty*, gave this preliminary definition of loyalty: "The willing and practical and thorough-going devotion of a person to a cause." He continued with a single sentence exegesis: "A man is loyal when, first, he has some *cause* to which he is loyal; when, secondly, he *willingly and thoroughly* devotes himself to the cause; and when, thirdly, he expresses his devotion in some *sustained and practical* way, by acting steadily in the service of his cause." Royce's final definition of loyalty is "Loyalty is the Will to Believe in something eternal, and to express that belief in the practical life of a human being."[9] William James had argued that where there is a genuine option, that is, an option that is "living, forced, and momentous, that cannot by its nature be decided on intellectual grounds, our passional nature not only lawfully may but must decide."[10] Both Royce and James were arguing for a primary role of will in both decision making and practical expression.

Our sample would support these positions. For example, God was an intellectual problem for one man, involving him in a ten to fifteen year period of vacillation between belief and doubt. His had been a devout home in which the Christian way of viewing things seemed natural and unproblematic. In military service he bumped into world views very different from his. It was during these years that he had his one and only mystical experience. Such was the context for his intellectual struggles. He asserted that all the while he struggled he "was a believer at least in the sense of wanting to be a believer. If intellectual honesty left open the reasonable possibility of belief, I was likely to keep pushing at the door, so to speak." While he was trying to put pieces together, there was a deeper level of faith that had not declined since "he was passionately [the very word used by James] concerned about such matters." But his passional concern created new problems. As he put it, "Naturally, I was very suspicious of believing things because I wanted to believe them, and that works an opposite kind of dynamic, making one skeptical of one's own belief. If they [beliefs] conform to what you want to believe, you have all the more reason to be doubtful about them." The rich description furnished by our friend is atypical. But the struggle for belief and the role of the will in believing is not atypical. Among many there was a passional pushing at the door of belief. As a woman put it, "Ultimately, there is a willing to believe and a not willing to believe. There is the mystery of the will. Belief requires an act of will at a primary level."

The role of will can be put biblically as obedient hearing, that is, as response to the claims of God. Alan Richardson makes the claim that Paul's favorite way of describing faith is as an obedient response to Jesus Christ. For Paul, faith is "the 'yes' of the whole personality to the fact of Christ."[11] Faith is associated with hearing, and hearing with obedience. This is the most common way our study saw commitment: as an act in response to an action of God. It might be as seemingly simple as to be willing to repeat the good news. Witnessing or confessing, as one observed, is an essential act of faith in response to the Christian message. Surrender, not a crumbling of the will but an intentional activity in which the self is placed at the behest of divine purposing, marked our subjects.

The horizontal direction commitment took was toward people. The horizontal concern was judged to be not merely a humanistic response but a response to God. Our interviewees were trying to respond to human need as a basic way of being faithful to God. Of course, psychological needs (i.e., the need to be needed) were operative also. What we did not find was an obsessive need, a need giving rise to rescue fantasies, a need dominated by ego hunger. They identified what they were doing as a response to what they had heard—the gospel. They would affirm Franz Bidder's definition of faith "as pledge, that is, as a tying of oneself, a betrothing of oneself, and entering into covenant."[12] The covenant into which they entered, itself a voluntaristic move, included obligations, obligations that did not feel onerous to our subjects because they were responding to a grace-act that created the covenant and included them. In covenantal language, they were hearing and struggling to be obedient. They were trying to target their obedience toward their human fellows. Theirs was willed love, as they concentrated on responding to the gospel in actions as appropriate as possible to the moment of need. Those who told us about themselves would be embarrassed by even the suggestion that they had gained anything like Kierkegaard's purity of heart, that is, willing one thing. But it is our estimate that that was the way their wills were bent.

Risk Taking

Many of our subjects spoke specifically of commitment as risk taking. Many of these interviews corroborated John Cobb's words that faith is a "continual challenge to do and dare . . . and to venture out beyond the limits laid down by the past."[13] In commitment, the will is pitched forward toward new possibilities. Every commitment goes beyond the past in the direction of the future. The picture we have in mind is of the runner leaning forward into the next moment. This is the posture of the faith commitment. Faith is always somewhat off balance as it ventures forward into the new. And the new contains risk. Two interviewees make the point for the rest.

A woman raised the question, "Can my faith stand the test in the marketplace?" The metaphor is interesting and significant. "Marketplace" suggests the risking of capital. The one who used the marketplace metaphor had in mind the investment of faith at some risk. For, as she observed, it either works or you give it up. She was no more neutral than a businessman investing his capital. She was insisting that faith must be tested by whether it meets human needs. That was the meaning of "marketplace": a place where fanatical caring goes on, demanding everything of the carer, with all the risks implicit and explicit in such caring. She felt it was just here that the laity are cheated. Few are ever dared to risk their faith in caring. A businessman may become a trustee of an ecclesiastical institution, but he is rarely dared to test his faith in serving his employees in the radical meaning of love. For this woman, risking meant putting one's faith to the test, which might reveal that the faith as held is not working.

A pastor who said that his faith tells him he must get involved with people quite naturally saw faith as risk taking. He knew that to get involved with people is to run risks. Yet any other kind of life, he thought, was only half-living. "Life only gets to be exciting when you get out there beyond your depths, where you cannot do it all by yourself." Whether he had in mind Kierkegaard's analogy of being alone in seventy thousand fathoms of water, we do not know. But he felt keenly the risk, for it was in this context that he made a statement about prayer: "If you're living without prayer, then you're not living. I can't take the kind of risks I take without prayer and the sense of the sustaining God who will pick you up when you fall on your face, as you are bound to do." His risk taking was theologically grounded: "God takes risks, too." What he had in mind was both the freedom God gave to human beings and the incarnation whereby God engaged the divine self with that freedom, at such awful cost. Our friend was decisive about following his incarnational theology into the risk-places. He would not have it otherwise. "If you are safe, something is wrong; you are missing something."

We were impressed by how many identified with Abraham in his never settling down. Abraham, a paradigm of trust, was also a paradigm of commitment. He set out beyond road signs, charting new territory. Some of our company used the Abrahamic saga to epitomize their reaching beyond their grasp. The fear of some was of being tamed by the culture. They were talking about risking out of loyalty to an ultimate concern: "in spite of consequences."

Ownership

So far we have looked at commitment as an act of will incurring risk. Now we must ask whose commitment this is, which is the question of ownership. It is ownership that seems to be at the core of commitment, as far as our study is concerned. An engineer put it whimsically, using an analogy of children building their own playhouse. "It may be skewed, the nails awry, but it's theirs. If parents rebuild it for them, more often than not the children won't touch it. It's not their dream; it's sterile. It's got to be theirs. Each must build his own house in his own way, molding it as he goes along. Faith is not good if it is imposed or transmitted. Then it's not yours. Like a playhouse, it's only good if it's yours."

Common to over 90 percent of the interviewees was a sense of struggle. At bottom the struggle was over identity. Whose faith is this? Who am I as a person of faith? To these two questions our sample volunteered strong convictions. They showed throughout the interviews that the question of faith identity was central not only to their religious lives but to their personal identities.

A professor voiced it in these words: "Passion is crucial for me. What we are dealing with is not first intellectual fascination but life or death. If I break faith, I break that which gives me my identity. I'd have to figure out some other way to organize my life." For him as for many others, faith has a celebrative dimension about it: it celebrates life pitched toward God and all the while it celebrates a personal identity being shaped by the God up ahead. The faith enterprise is a convicted thing around which is woven the strands of a life in process. Ownership is never signed, sealed, and delivered. It is always in the process of being claimed. These people were living out ahead, determining who they were as they negotiated one passage after another. They owned a large commitment that in turn owned them. They filled in the blanks as they went along.

Implicit from beginning to end in at least three-quarters of the interviews was a rugged sense of the need to be free and to be responsible. The need to be free was the need to achieve freedom out of the possibility of freedom. The need to be responsible was the need to lay a claim, to act out of a center that had made an ultimate commitment, to be accountable. Within creaturely limitations, our sample embraced the fundamental notion that they were finally responsible for what they were. A few gave credit to Gestalt psychology for helping them to see and conceptualize this; a few others came to it out of other types of therapy. But most achieved the insight out of their reading of the script of their journeying how they had come to be where they were. Almost all would affirm that *how* they put things together through the moments and the days of their years is *what* they are. It was theirs, for better or for worse. The directionality of their lives, that is, the ordering of their commitments so that the ordering developed a pattern, they acknowledged to be theirs. While we heard criticism of parents, homes, churches, colleagues, educational experiences, and so on, and while we became aware of their regret for what might have been, we never sensed that any located final responsibility for their own lives outside of themselves. This had basic meaning for commitment, because they saw their lives as a process of much turning, winnowing, sharpening, deciding, acting, arranging, and rearranging, all in the direction of what they thought was ultimate. The processive note is picked up in the words of one: "I think faith is a kind of victory that has to be won every day." The faith identity of the self is the precipitate of the daily struggle. In the context of faith, when they took aim by their commitments they were at the same time targeting their own selfhoods.

Gordon W. Allport and J. Michael Ross are responsible for discerning the distinction between extrinsic and intrinsic religion. According to them, those who are extrinsically religious use religion as a means to an end: security, status, comfort. Religion then has utilitarian value. Religion in this mode is dependency religion; that is, the extrinsically religious depend on religious formulation or ritual, for example, as a crutch. Those who are intrinsically religious live their religion; it is crucial to, or at the center of, their lives. Such people internalize it; they make it their own. If they have a need for crutches, it is minimal.[14] Religion in this mode is ownership as we have been describing it. While one would expect some variation within either mode, at least three-fourths of our sample were found located within the intrinsic mode. In the economy of their lives, their ultimate loyalty intrinsically formed who they were.

A humble statement by a professional describes the total point of commitment: "The terror of my life is that I might come to the moment of dying and have the feeling that my life was not useful to God. Yet I have no need to try to assure that I am successful. I have only the need to give the best that I have, knowing that God will do with what I do for good. That's the high calling to which my life endeavors to respond."

Faith as Belief

If it ever needed documentation, Anselm's famous dictum that faith seeks understanding is confirmed by our small study.[15] Anselm meant by faith primarily a movement of the will, that is, an obedient loving response to God. It is this faith, a prior datum, that inherently seeks to understand itself.[16] Behind theology, which is faith's understanding, is faith as trust and commitment.

From our study we have concluded that trust and commitment are basic forms of faith and, as such, that they are the salvific forms of faith. Salvation is not dependent on belief, certainly not on correct or orthodox belief, although belief does inform and enhance trust and commitment. Trust and commitment are more relational forms of faith. Salvation is at the relational level. Belief, at least minimally, tries to understand the salvific-relational level of faith. In our study we cannot discern any significant difference at the trust and commitment levels between the laity and the professionals. The difference is markedly at the belief level.

Our professional sample was reflectively and profoundly involved in belief formation. We are identifying belief as the theological struggle to understand what trust and commitment mean. Of sixty professionals interviewed, fifty-nine emphasized the belief form of faith, while less than 20 percent of the laypeople did so. Those who did emphasize belief seemed to presuppose trust and commitment as impelling them to wrestle cognitively with that which undergirded them and aimed them in a given direction. They would wholeheartedly agree with Barth: "It is my very faith itself that summons me to knowledge."[17] It was clear throughout the interviews that the rational side of faith, exciting as it was, was to explicate something deeper.

Faith Seeking Understanding

For the professionals, rational inquiry seemed to take place within two concentric circles. The inner circle represents faith as the irreducible precipitate left by home, church, significant others, religious experience—

in short, the spiritual autobiography. One said of this precipitate, "I have questioned faith deeply, but in the context of itself. Of its own importance it itself has demanded to be questioned. There's a reality that's just present, a deep trust working itself out." What was present for all was the "heart of faith," a stubborn given. Strenuous theological work it was, to unwrap what was in the heart. The unwrapping process was faith as trust and commitment seeking to understand itself both in its depths and its concentricity.

The outer circle represents the myriad daily and hourly experiences to which faith must relate. Among the professionals faith was no carefully defended enclave, except for perhaps two persons. It had to face the outer circle. Reason moved back and forth between the "heart of faith" and the rest of life's experiences. In other words, our interviewees were not doing armchair theology out of the givens of their faith. The belief role of faith was playing itself out between the interiorized faith of trust and commitment and the many engagements with the physical and social realities that environed each person.

There was the inner compulsion to think out what one's own faith meant, but in the context of the circle of total experience. Belief making was constantly engaged in bringing meaning to the facts of experience as the facts instructed belief where to look. As some pointed out, belief was always in passage, that is, in some state of flux, for it always had new data upon which to reflect. We found very little hardened theological formulation. That does not mean that there were no strong positions. But faith reflection was the struggle to understand theologically in the context of lived experience. A set of beliefs could be construed as a map for the trip, but there was an awareness that sometimes the trip might rewrite the map.

Stages Along the Way: Three Forms of Faith

One pastor said, "The agenda of faith is life." For example, he noted how his wife and children gave his life a value structure, a quality of richness, purpose, and happiness. These were only illustrative for him of the richness of experience that had to be correlated with faith. He was thus opposing a spiritual narcissism in which faith is engaged in merely intramural activity, and also opposing lighting up the landscape of life with a fifteen-watt bulb when one could light it with the divine light intent on overcoming the darkness. He was pressing for a dialectic between a few firmly held givens on which he had put his money and life situations on which he was spending the interest on his money. At stake for him was the survival of the human spirit. That spirit he wanted rescued from any narrow-gauge view of what Christ is in our life to do. His struggle for meaning was to defend the human spirit against becoming ingrown through narrowness. In his words, "If we can defend the human spirit and keep it from being corrupted, I think we can cope with the future." He thought Christian theology's task was to save the spirit by helping to provide a transcendent set of meanings by which to inform the human pilgrimage. But at the same time he knew that that pilgrimage would have its effect on theology. For him, preaching is faith examining itself in the context of the congregation's lived experience, thus helping both the congregation and the preacher to formulate belief that is in touch with daily life.

Another pastor led us in the search for understanding from a somewhat different perspective. He had become less theoretical and more experiential in the parish. It was the experiential that drove him to question his commitments, not out of doubt but out of the need for illuminating insight. The insight he was searching for was how to cope theologically with the problem of evil. Albert Camus' *The Plague* had first nagged him to contemplate what kind of a God one can believe in given the absurdity of evil, as Camus saw it. Then his pastoral experiences drove him to agonize over what his own faith could say to the problem of evil. In wrestling with this problem, his view of God turned from a God who could do everything to a God very much embattled in the struggle with evil and affected by that struggle. His new formulation concluded that God could not be omnipotent precisely because evil had terrible power of its own.

If the professors were less affected by the congregational milieu than pastors, they nevertheless had lived experience forcing them, too, to be constantly working on their theological agendas. One said, "I think, if I were to write the autobiography of my faith, it would be along these lines: most of my theology has developed in my experience and my interaction with people. And then my thinking about theology is a way of trying to give some kind of articulation to that, and to understand it, and to come to terms with it in a more integrative way." He illustrated this with a moving experience with his mother. She had had a breakdown, occasioning a deep, lengthy depression. In corresponding with her, he felt he could not use the fundamentalist language his mother preferred and maintain his integrity. There was great theological distance between them. Many of her letters were filled with testimonials designed to be manipulative. Finally, his mother was not eating, not communicating. He had a choice: maintain this fancied integrity and miss her or communicate in language she could understand. He wrote a letter using all the traditional language to remind her of her faith and to say he cared. A letter came back that never said one word of theology; it just said straightforwardly where she was: okay. She no longer had a need to convert him. This touching exchange opened up for him afresh what incarnation was about: real presence and caring in terms of human understandability with salvific intent. This became his paradigm for understanding Christian theology anew. As a consequence his concept of God had changed from an external, controlling God to a God immanent in life's process and sharing the divine Self in every need.

It is as though theology had to have experiential references to have meaning—that God-talk must refer to something in the world that in itself discloses meaning. Neither professors nor pastors were ivory tower figures, with one exception. They were capable of remarkable abstraction and sometimes brilliant conceptualization, but always between two poles: some givens of their faith and concrete lived experiences. Belief formation was not the base of faith. In fact, faith was obviously deeper than any understanding developed on that faith. Belief formation was reason's attempt to clarify the meaning of the dialogue between the poles. Thus belief was answering to one of the deepest needs of the human spirit, as Paul Tillich has shown: the need for meaning.

Our interviewees were trying to make some sense out of the vast multiplicity of experience. They did this through powerful images, especially creation and re-creation, Exodus and Resurrection, as these focused on redemption and liberation. Perhaps it is a sign of the times that our sample returned again and again to images of redemption, especially in terms of Resurrection and Exodus. We cite as an example one who noted that central to her father's theology was the overruling power of God. She turned that notion of power to a different understanding of power: a redemptive power that spends and risks itself. Her belief in Resurrection was affirmation that God continues to give of the divine Self and is not finally destroyed by crucifixion. She maintained continuity with her roots while creating her own novelty of interpretation that emphasized a divine assurance of victory. Along the way, a sense of deity was formed that was somewhat different from a traditional omnipotence. But there was power to effect a new creation out of the pain and suffering of the old, and the image for this new creation was Resurrection. "Behold, I am making all things new" was her chosen text.

Among the professional sample, and in a few of the laity, doubt seemed to be indigenous to the struggle for an adequate conceptuality that would stand up to experience. This does not make experience the sole test of truth, but it does demand that a conceptuality be adequate to cope cognitively with experience and coherent enough to display some inner consistency and harmony. The theological struggle was to develop a belief system that would do justice to the diversity of experience. These were intellectually gifted men and women whose minds kept probing for clearer meaning and richer syntheses. They seemed driven to cognitive resolution of hard theoretical problems. These people had experiential trust and commitment. The doubt was part of the intellectual struggle to understand how that which was trusted and which commanded their loyalty was related to space and time. Earlier conceptions of God were often inadequate. They were searching for a theological position that could do justice to their direct religious intuitions and also elucidate common experience. The struggle was to examine faith in the context of lived experience without trivializing either faith or the rest of human experience. Doubt was the painful concern as to whether one could believe or not believe without trivializing hard questions.

Those who talked most about doubt were aware that *something* allowed the doubt. Perduring through the questioning was a fundamental intuition, which we are calling trust. Faith itself demanded the questioning. The one we quoted at length on trust was also insightful on doubt. "It has come to me that doubt is almost a necessary precondition to faith. Yet doubt presupposes the presence of something that allows, even encourages, the doubt. Faith served as the ground by which I was able to raise the doubt and ask the question. Doubt and faith presuppose each other. The Given enables one to almost formulate the question, or the nay-saying, or the doubt. This perdured through the doubt. I never found myself doubting unto despair, but I did find myself living through the doubting." Like this believer, those doubting seemed to find doubt, while painful, a zest and an enrichment to the process of belief formation as well as self-formation.

The laypersons' doing of theology paled sadly against the richness of the professionals' forming of beliefs. Fewer than twenty-five did much theological wrestling. However, those who went on to graduate school in whatever field seemed to evidence more interest in struggling with belief formation. As we have already noted, our lay sample was atypical in the number of college graduates and the number of those who had earned some graduate school degree. Of the 150 laypeople studied, 39 percent were college graduates, and another 21 percent had earned degrees at the master's or doctoral level. These totaled 60 percent. (It has intrigued us why so many pastors selected their faithful people from the ranks of higher education. We did not learn about their educational levels until well into the interviews.) Four important considerations emerged out of this educational overbalance. First, there is no discernible difference between the 39 percent who graduated from college and the 40 percent who did not go to college, so far as doing theology is concerned. Frankly, this was a surprising and discomfiting finding. We had surmised that college would at least prompt intellectual curiosity and help to pose problems from the natural or social sciences or from the liberal arts to initiate theological thinking. College did not seem to provide that impetus. The raw stuff of lived experience did for some, but college did not seem to broaden the theological inquiry or even furnish the tools for meaningful discourse.

The second consideration is that those who went to graduate school did seem to want to do some struggling with their intellectual beliefs. But we were not able to ascertain whether the graduate school experience prodded this struggling or whether those who did go on in their higher education had a deeper innate curiosity that impelled them to seek further education in the first place. Here curiosity is meant to suggest something of a thirst for knowledge and a built-in desire to think through such questions as lived experience poses for theology.

The third consideration is that even the laypeople who had done some theological questioning of their faith as trust and commitment and who were struggling somewhat toward a deeper understanding demonstrated three basic deficiencies: (1) a paucity of resources, primarily biblical and the theological and historical traditions, with which to inform their seeking understanding; (2) a lack of depth, as though whatever probings they had done or were doing were at levels not satisfying to themselves; and (3) an ignorance of theological method for thinking theologically, that is, from the perspective of God whom they trusted and to whom they were committed about their lived experience.

The fourth consideration is that the laity seemed hampered by having little or no theological language. Every discipline requires a language with which to think as well as to articulate meanings. The laity in our study, if they used theological terms, seemed ill at ease with them. This may have limited their theological reflection, or at least their articulation of any theological meaning they were living with. For instance, Christ, Jesus, Spirit, Lord were vaguely identified. The name "Lord" seemed to be a catch-all for any reference to deity, whether God, Christ, or Spirit, and was used as an inclusive pointing word. The relation of Jesus to Lord, God, Christ, Spirit came off as confused. A second illustration is that the concept of sin had a decidedly moralistic bent to it, barely if at all informed by a biblical understanding of sin. These two illustrations center around crucial theological beliefs within the Christian tradition. We return to the need for theological language in the next chapter.

If the eighty-plus percent in our lay sample who did not show much interest in seeking a deeper theological understanding of their faith are representative of the laity across the church, might that partly account for the relatively closed Bible, the low estate of the sacraments, the constricted scope and depth of prayer, the restricted ethical perspective, and the quite limited place of the sermon? For example, if theology gives the worshiper a clearer understanding of the sacraments, that understanding would seem to enhance their value each time either sacrament becomes the focus of worship. If the pastor knows that there are biblically informed and theologically alert congregants sitting in the pews awaiting the sermon, that should be some motivation for the pastor to make his or her office into a *study* for the preparation of the sermon as well as all other teaching and proclaiming occasions.

If our study is an even fairly accurate perception of the faith life of the church, the professionals make a major effort to do theology while the laity make at best a minor effort. Faith needs understanding for the sake of worshiping God more truly and serving the Divine with more discipline, which is discipleship. If the following diagram even fairly accurately suggests the functioning of the church within the concentric circles, as it moves from the heart of the church as a gathered worshiping community to the outreach of the church as scattered, the weak spot of belief formation would seem to demand of the church a total commitment to education with new intensity at the adult stages.

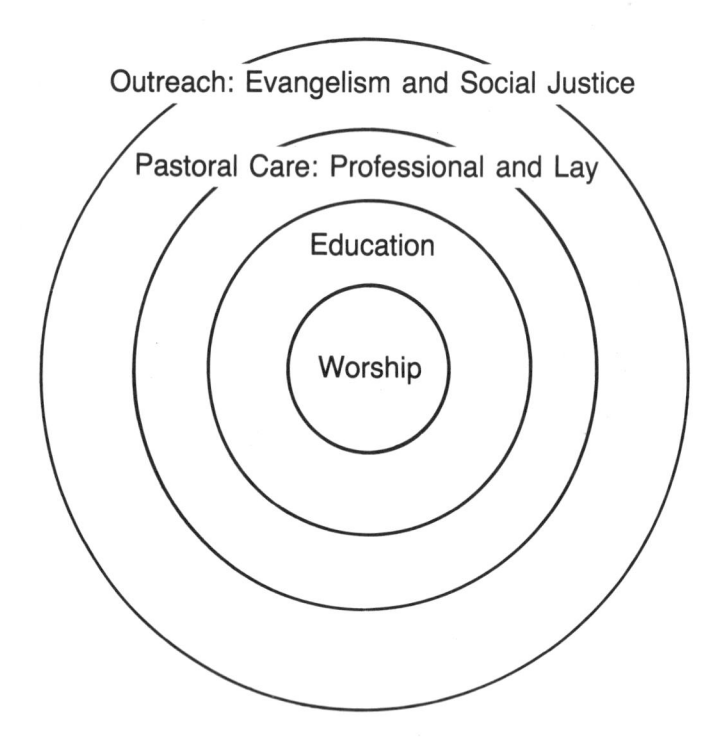

Outreach: Evangelism and Social Justice

Pastoral Care: Professional and Lay

Education

Worship

Worship provides a communal experience with the Holy One. Education seeks to understand that experience, especially the One in whom trust is placed and to whom commitment is made. Pastoral care moves out to minister to those in personal need, including crisis times. Outreach means the gospel is seeking the lost sheep (evangelism) and redeeming the structures of injustice wherever they may be (ethics).

We intend no indictment of laity on these pages except

to wonder about their intellectual or cognitive commitment to becoming at least good amateur theologians in their own right. And commitment is at the base of motivation. But there is certainly an implied indictment of the professional leadership of the church for its failure to perform the rabbinic or teaching role, not so much of transmitting information as of being a Socratic midwife in helping at least a good portion of the congregation to become good lay theologians. It is difficult to think of a greater mission than enabling the church to become theologically literate. Therefore, it is as difficult to think of a more apparent failure than to fail to fulfill that mission.

Education would seem to be essential to the church's total life, not just to overcome biblical and theological illiteracy but also to enable the church to be about its servant functions in the world. Doing theology by the laity and professionals is for the sake of the ministry of God in the world. In some of the following chapters, especially 5 through 9, some detailed suggestions are made within various contexts, for example, Bible, prayer.

In this chapter we have been observing that the forms of faith are activities and states of each person as he or she relates to the stuff of life. Trust is a visceral form, relating to the feeders of life; commitment is a willed form, responding to penultimate and ultimate objects of trust; belief is a form of cognitive response to what trust has felt and commitment obeyed. Belief is faith standing on tip-toe to ferret out the meaning of what is going on. Salvation is at the trust and commitment levels; belief is to understand as clearly as possible what that salvation means. Faith is an organismic term describing a religious Vision and giving direction to the soul to channel its intention to live toward that Vision.

NOTES

1. H. Richard Niebuhr, *The Responsible Self* (New York: Harper, 1963), p. 118.
2. For a full treatment of Erikson's stage one, see Erik H. Erikson, *Childhood and Society*, rev. ed. (New York: Norton, 1963), pp. 247-51.
3. Robert McAfee Brown, *Is Faith Obsolete?* (Philadelphia: Westminster, 1974).
4. Olivier A. Rabut, *Faith and Doubt*, tr. by Boume and William Whitman (New York: Sheed and Ward, 1967), pp. 99, 100.
5. Artur Weiser, *Theological Dictionary of the New Testament*, tr. by Geoffrey Bromiley, vol. 6 (Grand Rapids: Eerdmans, 1968), p. 196.
6. Alan Richardson, *An Introduction to the Theology of the New Testament* (New York: Harper, 1958), p. 19.
7. C. H. Dodd, *The Epistle of Paul to the Romans* (New York: Harper, n.d.), pp. 70, 71.
8. Martin Buber, *The Eclipse of God* (New York: Harper, 1952), pp. 106-7.
9. Josiah Royce, *The Basic Writings of Josiah Royce*, vol. 2, ed. by John J. McDermott (Chicago: University of Chicago Press, 1969), pp. 861, 997.
10. William James, *The Will to Believe and Other Essays in Popular Philosophy and Human Immortality* (New York: Dover, 1956), pp. 3, 11.
11. Richardson, *Introduction*, p. 24.
12. As quoted by Martin Buber, *Mamre*, tr. by Greta Hort (Melbourne: Melbourne Union Press, 1946), p. 19.
13. John B. Cobb, Jr., *God and the World* (Philadelphia: Westminster, 1969), p. 83.
14. Gordon W. Allport and J. Michael Ross, "Personal Religious Orientation and Prejudice," *Journal of Personality and Social Psychology* 5, no. 4 (1967): 432-43.
15. The original title of his *Proslogium* was *Faith Seeking Understanding*. Anselm, *Proslogium* (La Salle, Ill.: Open Court, 1948), p. 2.
16. Cf. Karl Barth, *Anselm* (Cleveland: World, 1961), pp. 16ff.
17. Ibid., p. 18.

CHAPTER · 2

Human Needs: Clamorings for Faith

Throughout the lengthy process of interviewing 210 faithful people, a psychologist, Abraham Maslow, kept emerging and reemerging in our consciousness. It was Maslow who carefully correlated human needs with motivation.[1] But it was not his hierarchy of needs that was front and center; rather, it was his careful analysis of how human needs are profound motivators for human reaches and human behaviors. In this chapter we shall look briefly at some human needs that surfaced in our sample as motivators toward faith, whether as trust, commitment, or belief. We isolate six needs.

The Need to Cope with Lived Experience, Especially Crisis

Wartime foxholes, illness (both one's own and loved ones'), death in the family and among friends, divorce, job loss, repetitive labor, anguish over children's serious destructive behavior, church fights and church pettiness, being female, being black—in short, the continuum of human experience forced faith to interrogate itself by new doubting, to renew its trusting at a deeper level, and, among nearly all the professionals and almost

20 percent of the laypeople, to reformulate beliefs to account for such events within the crucible of lived experience. One put it simply for the many: "In the midst of all this my faith has been formed."

The uncle of a laywoman was choked to death by a black man. The minister of her aunt, the widow, said, "Don't blame the race for what one man did. There's a lot of understanding that needs to take place between the races." So her aunt became involved with black people and their culture. She got a job teaching in a black college. Said this interviewee, "I have these kinds of examples of what the Christian faith leads people to."

One of the theologically articulate laywomen found her faith challenged by the fact of change itself. Dramatic changes, some of which crumpled her world, brought into her consciousness the notion that life is always changing, which prompted her to question the place of God within an ever-changing universe. She had come to this conclusion, helped by the Bethel Bible study: "I must trust that God has a plan for reconciling the world to himself. God is the Victor, the Director of the world. Sometimes you wonder where God is in the picture. But if God is not in the picture, neither are we, for we are a part of God. You know through your faith that God is working in the world, though it's hard to understand how that is at times. That's my motivation to keep studying and learning. I'm open to change even if it is painful, as it has been."

No experience put to faith the question that death did. The laity and professionals alike struggled with that question. And both laid it partly to rest in deepened trust. A number of professionals expressed that resolution in belief statements reformulated to deal with the question, three of which we share.

A professor painfully worked through the death of his

three-year-old. One day the infant was alive and well, the next morning dead in his crib. Reflected the father to us, "To this day I struggle with this question, maybe the most momentous of all: how is God related to this creation? Is God weak or is he mighty? I have a very difficult time acknowledging God as almighty. In fact, I resent prayers that begin 'Almighty God.' It's not just my son but other similar situations. People talk easily and glibly about the will of God. Death is not God's will, but life. The world is simply absurd. Faith must struggle with that. The answer for me is to overcome absurdity by deeds of love, kindness, mercy. My trust is in this tremendous God who shares his God-ness with us, as he did with Jesus, in the midst of this absurd life, motivating those deeds of love."

The daughter of one of the interviewees died at twenty-one. Through his grief work he came to articulate anew his faith, and in that struggle thought he had become a more total human being. He sensed a new linkage with the human situation through his losing and mourning. He became more accepting of the world on its terms. Through this tragedy his faith stretched toward a new expression. In his own language, "God would be less than good to us if he never let us cry or fail or if we were never allowed to be bewildered by death."

Another pastor took a symbolic journey. A close friend had shot himself. In the midst of that death he had to come to grips with his own dying. Only as he could come to let himself die could he let his friend die. In the midst of wrestling with his friend's death and his own, aided by some Gestalt training, his faith was verified for him. He said very simply, "I believe in the love of Christ in the midst of those kinds of things. I was then able to take my friend's young son and we climbed a mountain and at the top we proclaimed life. That's the good news."

The Need for Intimate Spiritual Friends

The following two chapters testify to how profoundly the human community impacts faith. In this section we are looking at the need for spiritual intimacy within the human community, a need evident in the total sample, with no exceptions. It was as though this need, while reaching for human spiritual intimacy, was using the human to advance to the Divine. A spiritual friend might serve the need, further the need, or at times shoot it down, only for it to rise again in relentless search for ultimate spiritual fulfillment. In its most transcendent form, the need seems to agree with Augustine's often quoted confession: "For Thou madest us for Thyself, and our heart is restless, until it repose in Thee."

The need for spiritual intimacy was expressed in the desire for a few, perhaps only two or three, spiritual friends. The need emerged as pastors talked regretfully of shallow or non-existent collegial relationships. Professors almost unanimously bemoaned a similar experience with their colleagues, except at the non-confessional cognitive level. Some of the laity found some of their deepest spiritual satisfactions in small support groups gathered for Bible study, as we will note in chapter 4. Sadly, the professionals most often did not find this need for spiritual intimacy met in the congregation, perhaps part of the price of the tragic hiatus that continues to exist between clergy and laity. (We wonder if this still obtains between younger clergy and laity?)

As we listened to the interviewees, we heard a yearning for something beyond a social grouping with whom to enjoy getting together. This yearning was not for more social support to fund the basic need for affection, as Karen Horney, the psychoanalyst, terms it. Social togetherness, however rich, would not necessarily satisfy this need. It was the need for an unusual kind of human friendship that would aid the human spirit in its journey toward the divine Spirit. It was a yearning for intimacy with one or two others so that spiritual growth, that is, growth toward transcendent Value, might continue.

This particular need was not for more friends but for a certain kind or quality of friend, for a soul-brother or soul-sister who could be part of a continuing quest for the ultimate social intimacy. What comes to mind is the Spiritual Director or Spiritual Guide in the Roman Catholic tradition. While the Protestant preference might be for the terminology "spiritual friend," for egalitarian reasons, some content from the role of spiritual director or guide is the kind of intimacy this need seeks. For example, a spiritual friend would encourage the living of one's spiritual vocation, help further the search for the Mind of Christ, lift up the love of neighbor by encouraging greater sensitivity to fellow human beings, and spur the search for *shalom*, that is, for integration and wholeness. Pastors might well consider becoming a spiritual friend to a few when the conditions are appropriate. But they might do better to arrange training opportunities for laypeople to become in a self-conscious way such a soul-brother or sister. Two resources for such training are Tilden Edwards, *Spiritual Friend, Reclaiming the Gift of Spiritual Direction* (New York: Paulist, 1980) and Thomas Merton, *Spiritual Direction and Meditation* (Collegeville, Minn.: Liturgical Press, 1960).

The Need to Be Accepted

About a third of our total sample stressed their need just to be accepted, that is, accepted as a person—the freedom to be without a threatening sense of impending judgment. One who found such acceptance put it epigrammatically: "I finally got the sense that it's okay to be me, warts and all." A professor of drama put the problem in terms of her upbringing: "My early church experience was on earning of salvation, as most fundamentalistic churches are. And at home Father was judgmental. He never punished me, but I always had the feeling that if I did this or that, Father wouldn't love me. Sometimes I still feel my father is going to get me, and he's been dead for thirteen years. I had my first glass of wine in Europe when I was twenty-two. That shook my world, because my world didn't collapse. However, I still needed psychotherapy to clarify the relation between God and my father, and to see God as loving and less judgmental."

Whether it was through psychotherapy, sensitivity training, good pastoral care, effective support groups, or some other therapeutic mode, some who talked about the need to be accepted had come to some acceptance of themselves and were living out that acceptance. They came to enjoy themselves, sometimes for the first time, and they understood better their motivations. They gained some integration of the self, rejected old manipulative techniques that were no longer working (if they ever did), became less adolescent in seeing life as white and black, good and evil, right and wrong, and overcame compulsive tendencies that made of life only a series of rituals. These inward journeys impacted their faith.

They were certain that they were more open: open to divine guidance; open to the nuances of divine initiative; open to the creation, especially the human creation, apart from which that guidance seemed partially blocked; and open to the deeper recesses (that is, the unconscious) of their own being, where for some, at least, God operated, the divine Spirit meeting theirs. They were also sure they were better *integrated:* the shadow-side of the person integrated with other aspects of life so that there was less need, for example, for one to deny that she "is a bitch at times," as a woman put it; less anxiety over possible eruptions of evil because it is dealt with all along; less need for pretension, and so more freedom to venture into risky areas as one tries to follow the divine leading. Finally, they were convinced that these were old needs that had been clamoring a long time for satisfaction and that had now been at least partially satiated. Those needs satisfied, faith could now blossom. Human need fulfillment at lower levels (e.g., safety and belongingness) enabled them to become more self-actualizing, after the model of Maslow, and so to move into greater freedom to enjoy diversity and to be more accessible to the good things God was always providing. One who objectified this content to us classified himself as theologically conservative but liberal in the sense of being open to the stirrings of the Divine in the world around. He felt himself both in touch with his roots, which were heavy and restrictive, and at the same time with his new being, which was "opening as a flower in the warm and encouraging sun." As one woman said, whose need to be accepted had been partially met, "It just grows your faith."

The Need to Define Oneself

An engineer gave us this judgment: "Everyone must somehow be shaped by his faith as well as shape his faith within his orbit of experience." One need seemed to surface about mid-way through practically every interview: it was the need to define oneself, to take charge of the shaping of oneself, to put oneself together. Only one person used the language of Maslow, namely, self-actualization, but at least in part that is what all 210 people had in mind: within the milieu of their lives they had to, and really wanted to, be responsible for defining who they were. All 210 people were relatively strong, centered people—centered not in the sense of their lives curving around themselves, but centered in the sense of putting themselves together and working out from who they were to the world environing them.

A black professor illustrated the fundamental point we are making through an experience he shared with us. His father as a young man had been struck by a white man, and had wondered if he should retaliate. If he did, the white man would be defining him. He would be merely reacting. He walked away choosing to define himself and his future. He recited this to his son—our friend—to encourage him to let no one on the outside define him. From within he should define who he was to himself. Said this friend, "I do define myself. Even a system is limited in its ability to negate me."

Our interviewees were everlastingly at the project of weaving old and new together to form the tapestry of their being. Out of the vast multiplicity of life they were at least partly aware of determining their selfhood. With some zest as well as anxiety, they were aware of responding to an obviously deep need. The struggle for self-definition was difficult and painful. One felt he was confronted with two options, one masculine, one feminine. The masculine option emphasized winning, intruding, overwhelming; the feminine, gentleness, flowing with life, responding to needs and processes instead of imposing one's own agenda. Part of his lifetime had been spent working through to what he called the feminine result.

We were impressed that most of our sample had a viable sense of being free. Often this was put in terms of liberation: liberation from a preoccupying "me," from social structures that are demeaning, from orthodoxies that are dead, from rituals that no longer have meaning, from theologies that are repressive, from selves that are only a tenth alive, from churches marking time, from life looking back, from painful guilt, from the need to win, from society's vulgar expectations, from nasty, domineering dispositions, from duress to trivia, and so on. Whatever the bondage, the liberating dynamic was faith, faith that helped to define what the reality of being human looks like. It was faith's vision that stamped selfhood as the gift of God; that is, selfhood is in part the creation of God as God brings to bear upon the ever-moving self the divine vision. Therefore, "No one can finally determine your value," one argued, "but you and your Creator. People cram themselves into boxes that limit them, sell themselves short, become stunted human beings. Whereas we are free to build the inner world to reflect God's creative vision." Freedom was never quantified into how much or how little. By most if not all, it was assumed to be an ontological corollary to human existence: that is, part of what it is to be human is to be free. The final human responsibility is what to make of that freedom.

Of course, not all of these faithful people traveled by the same route in defining themselves. For the professionals and twenty-five of the laity, the cognitive role was very strong. But for all, conation was powerfully present as they willed to come to grips with who they wanted to be as men and women of faith. Though they confessed that their responses were too often erratic and sinful, no matter how many times they missed the mark their aim was to follow the guiding of God as they defined and redefined themselves.

The Need to Express the Self

Three-quarters of all the interviews ended with words from the interviewees such as these: "Thank you for coming and letting me share with you things I've never shared with anyone else, things I've not thought about for years, things I didn't know were in me, some things that made me want to cry. Thank you for letting me share with you the story of my faith." Not all people said all of this, but most said most of it. These people were doing us a rare service by entering into a bit of research we were doing. Of course, we were thankful, but they barely let us get that out, so eager were they to express their own gratitude. Why? What was going on in those interviews, within the privacy of their feelings? We think we know, and it can be told in the gratitude of a seventy-year-old man interviewed by a graduate student as part of the pilot project leading up to our study. As the graduate student was leaving him he said to her, "Thank you for coming. I've been a Baptist all my life, and no one ever asked me how it was with me and God. Preachers have told me from the pulpit, but no one ever asked me. Thank you for letting me share my faith with you. I can't thank you enough." Brushing aside the probable overstatement of this gentleman, in his enthusiasm to share himself, including his faith, with another, he was making a profound statement about the human need to express oneself. Language is a way of remembering, for it is the expression of one's past in one's present, both to oneself and to another. It is also a way of being creative, for it recognizes elements out of our past with possibilities that lie ahead in imaginative novelty.[2] Thus the seventy-year-old man dredged out of his memories, of which he had had no recent conscious recall, faith experiences that when shared with his listener became alive in perhaps quite new, even startling, ways. Language is creative, or can be.

How many of our sample said, "Gee, I hadn't thought of that in years," and paused to re-ingest what was said! And for many of these people, body language as well as linguistic testimony seemed to indicate that a quickening, a coming alive, was taking place. We could only conjecture to ourselves about what was happening. They corroborated now and then the inference we had made but not spoken: that there had been a flash of new insight, or a momentary delight, or even a momentary resolve.

Whatever the complete role of language in its expression of a person, it recovers our memories, it is creative of the future, and it bonds speaker and hearer in a common momentary experience. There is a profound need to tell, to share, to get it out. This is at least part of the urge to testify, to witness. It is part of the charismatic experience. It may be a deep religious need; it surely is a deep human need.

Some authorities argue that we only think in linguistic symbols, that language and thought create each other. For example, the philosopher Whitehead has written, "The souls of men are the gift from language to mankind." He suggests rewriting the Genesis account of the sixth day to read, "He gave them speech, and they became souls."[3] The soul withers without expression; expression is the lifeblood of the soul, helping it to remember and to imagine, to rise above itself on the wings of contemplation and ultimately of adoration. If this is so, language is necessary to thinking, and thinking is necessary to belief formation, that is, to doing theology. As we noted in the previous chapter, the laity fall far behind the professionals at the belief, or theologizing, level of faith. Might this be partly because the laity do not feel comfortable with theological terms or even religious terms? Every set of experiences has a vocabulary and a style in which those experiences are phrased, put together, and given some systematic ordering, from medicine to art to computer science to religion. Church history is replete with such a vocabulary. It can be learned, that is, made useful, only as the learner struggles with it and uses it, perhaps awkwardly at first, until some proficiency develops. Education within the churches would seem made to order to teach first the rudimentary and later the sophisticated use of language to frame religious experience and theological concepts. But not education that is primarily lecture. Church education would seem to be at its best when it helps the laity to do theology for the sake of growing souls whose trust and commitment dimensions are lifted up into the thought processes called beliefs, which in turn strengthen trust and commitment. Thus, a fully orbed faith might even more worthily magnify the Lord and praise the name of God.

There is also a second programmatic implication. Congregations might be afforded opportunity for the people to say to one another how it is with their faith. Perhaps once a year, maybe during Lent or Holy Week, a gathering might take place for sharing in pairs. Public sharing always runs the risk of staging, of ego-tripping, of blandishing. Rather, let those gathered be taught quickly and simply to share with one another their faith stories, without interruption from the one listening, and then let them pair off, preferably with someone they know less well, and let the two spend an hour together, each listening to the faith journey of the other. Then call all back for a simple closure of perhaps a hymn and a prayer. Such a time of sharing the unique journey of each should enrich the life of the total congregation and yet keep sacred the story of every person. Such sharing might elicit a profound thank you, as our study did—a thank you because the soul had another opportunity to grow stronger through eliciting memory and anticipation in the process of sharing.

The Need for Ultimacy

A simple question was asked interviewees toward the end of the interview: "What does going to church mean to you or do for you?" Frankly, we thought we might hear about the sermon, the music, seeing old friends. Old friends did figure prominently, as did music, but that was about all. And yet we kept sensing something else, mostly unspoken but pointed to, which a few examples may make clear. A Methodist woman said, "The whole worship service, for me, is built around prayer, by which I mean confrontation with the Divine." Said an engineer, "Sometimes the tiniest truth revealed to me makes such an enormous difference, and I share it with someone else and he or she could not care less. It seems so inconsequential; yet to me it is a revelation from God." Another woman, again a Methodist, said, "God manifests himself in so many ways and through so many diverse phenomena. God is bigger than all things and comes through all things. Oh, the infinite and fantastic variety in the way God comes! Through these experiences, it seems to me, God has been polishing my soul, like polishing a gem." This woman used the "I am" passages of the New Testament, which reflect the self-consciousness of Jesus, to carry her sense of the greatness and majesty of God. Said a thirty-five-year-old administrator, "I suppose there is a need, maybe a fear, that is making me reach out to touch something larger than I am. God made us with a kind of yearning that we would need him. It is God who makes you reach back and touch his hand. There is a permanence to that that transcends all the uncertainties. So they are survivable. This all seems to revolve around a need within me. And I'm excited. It's so completely novel to see the world from the perspective of God. The color and texture are more alive. There's a newness, a freshness I want never to go away. I guess it fulfills some deep need."

As is quite evident, these quotations move beyond "going to church" to Something compelling beyond church, Something that permeates the total dimension of life. What we thought we picked up around the question about "going to church" kept expanding with so many to a Something that became a confrontation. The professionals rarely related this sense of Presence, to which we are pointing, to any church service or to "going to church." But it was almost a universal testimony that they were part of Something large, immense, upon which they and all life finally depended. Two words gather up this universal testimony: Immensity and Grace. They sensed an Immensity that was friendly. The awesome Power was trustworthy. The Power was gracious.

We are not altogether clear on our extrapolation, but we are convinced that we heard a basic need being met, within the welter of lived experience, by an immense Power that was *ultimate*. There was Something obviously drawing laity and professionals alike, not only to worship, but to Itself. What we sensed we were hearing did not sound like demanding habit or duty. It sounded very much like Rudolph Otto's sense of the Holy, which would fit neither the category of morality or the category of rationality. It was as though there was a stirring of the numinous, that is, a sense of awe-ful Presence, to borrow from Otto, a stirring within the soul as though Something from beyond the self was rousing the self. That Something Otto describes in such words as Aweful, Hidden, Mystery, the Holy, Majesty, Wholly Other.[4] We have called this, the numinous sense, the human need for the Ultimate, and the Ultimate is God, the awesome Mystery confronting us. No one put it in Otto's terms, and we cannot be certain that Otto's classic treatment of the Holy is what our sample would identify with in their

Human Needs: Clamorings for Faith

encounter with God. But Otto's analysis came to mind throughout the interviews as though it might describe that to which these faithful people were pointing. If so, "going to church," among many other religious activities, would have at its innermost core the most profound confrontation or meeting the human self can know: the soul adventuring toward the Holy One who has already moved to meet the soul. If this is correct, the primary burden on worship is frightful: to encourage the possibility of a meeting between the soul and the Ultimate One. The call to worship is awesome, to be engaged in prayerfully, for "going to church" has the breathtaking possibility of the Divine-Human Encounter taking place. Perhaps this is what one woman was reaching for in these words: "I come to church to pull myself together out of the world and worldly places. I need to come back, sit quietly, to submit myself to the Presence. At best, church would be one big Gregorian chant to me." Considering this, one criterion for liturgy, including the sermon, perhaps would ask, Does this hour help meet the human need for ultimacy? And beyond the liturgy, the criterion should continue to interrogate other moments of our lives. Do we afford times and places that give the Holy One a better chance to gain our attention and to meet our need for ultimacy? For this need is tragically overlaid by the economies of living and by the surfeits of materialism and hedonism in our technological civilization. If this is so, our civilization is demonic, for it domesticates and turns to idolatry the profound need that helps to qualify the human being as "little less than God," the Psalmist's notion of the potential grandeur of the human being. The need to experience the Holy needs to be awakened in each, as it was for Isaiah in his vision "in the year that King Uzziah died" (Isa. 6), if faith is to have its eyes and ears opened so that its mouth can answer the voice of the Holy One.

NOTES

1. Abraham Maslow, *Motivation and Personality* (New York: Harper, 1954).
2. Cf. Alfred North Whitehead, *Modes of Thought* (New York: Capricorn, 1939), p. 46.
3. Ibid., p. 57.
4. Rudolf Otto, *The Idea of the Holy* (London: Oxford, 1923), chaps. 2–6.

CHAPTER · 3

The Return to Roots

The temptation in this chapter is to confine ourselves to the rich variety of responses our sample made in paying tribute to those people from whom they learned faith. We shall happily yield to the temptation to share flavor, content, and insight as our interviewees shared these with us (although we suffer in this from an embarrassment of riches, since we can use but a minute amount of what they shared with us). We shall let them make their case in their own words, first with regard to the home and then the local church. Then we shall suggest what constitutes caring people and ask whether the church can program toward their development.

Caring people are the number one informers and shapers of faith. Because they continued to be important far beyond childhood, we shall devote the following chapter also to their input. But childhood's experience of caring people laid the root system for much of what came after. Ninety percent of the interviewees began their stories by opening up their childhoods. They opened doors to their childhood homes as though inviting us into where it all began.

Sometimes it began with grandparents. Four grandparents impressed a New Englander with their commitment, but religious faith was not out front in their commitment. Rather, "providing the necessities of life for their families kind of rounded out their mission in life. A rocking chair was their first luxury. God provided through the earth for them. As a youngster I was in tune with them, with nature, with the earth. My grandfather was the first one who was close to me to die. I still remember the smile on his face when he died. I felt God spoke to me through that smile. I knew his moods, and I knew he died happy."

A professor likewise traced his roots back to a grandparent. The scene he recounted also took place around a grandfather's deathbed. The grandfather had always dedicated his fields to God before planting them, discussed his day with God before beginning it, and prayed to God as to an old friend. Now on his deathbed he gathered the family around. "I was eleven at the time," said our interviewee. "Grandfather said, 'We're going to sing me in.' He died on the third verse of 'Amazing Grace.' That symbolized the kind of faith that sustained that old bird, and that was the kind of atmosphere in which I grew up."

As one might expect, parents were most often crucially important to their children's faith. But their influence was perceived by their children in a fascinating variety of ways. We point to that variety with several illustrations. Said a thirty-five-year-old layman, "My father was very relational; he did everything with you. Father built into me a positive attitude toward life. Maybe all the positiveness I have been allowed to find in my own faith was transmitted to me by my father. Yet I wouldn't call my dad a religious person; he never emphasized religion, was never doctrinaire, never pushed things on me. Perhaps he provided the environment in which my faith became a participatory faith. How do I communicate to my child what my faith is all about without absolutizing or dogmatizing? I've got to provide the environment for the growing of her faith, as Dad did for me."

An engineer recounted, "I don't remember ever being separated from it [faith] because it was part of the home." He went on to elaborate, "Christian teachings were part and parcel of everyday life. Father would read the Sunday text upon which the preacher would preach, and we would all discuss it before and after church. Father could quote Luther's small catechism verbatim. I had utmost respect for both father and mother. They followed through on what they believed. We kids grew up with a set of expectations about neighbors and the community. If the yard looked bad, you'd trim it, partly for the sake of the neighbor. You didn't throw papers on the street, partly because of the community. All that was important to my spiritual growth. I was being taught accountability."

A Baptist layman pinpointed a nodal moment in his faith journey. When he was fifteen he overheard his mother saying to a friend that if she died, she knew she would be with the Lord in heaven. "That testimony turned me around. At that moment I felt I belonged to Christ. I knew you didn't earn heaven."

A forty-two-year-old Presbyterian related how his father was important to his faith in yet a different way. When he was in the primary grades his father told him he had to go to church. "Okay, Dad, for what reason?" he asked. His dad's answer: " 'The culture you are in is basically Christian: laws, social attitudes, mores. You can't operate effectively in this society unless you know what the society is all about. So go long enough to understand and make up your own mind about it [Christianity].' When it came time for communicants' class, I said I wasn't interested. My father's response: 'Take it; I don't care if you join or not, but do it. If you are so smart, get smarter.' It was my father's intellectual concern that nailed me. He was not a role model to me, but his intellectual honesty made the difference."

For one more, quite diverse, experience we turn to a lawyer whose father died before he was old enough to know him. "The way my mother and other people talked about my father, I came to think of him as a very special person. When I recited the Lord's Prayer at night, I actually thought it was to my father I was praying—not to God or to the Lord. It seemed so natural." Much later, in retrospect, he came to locate his faith yearnings within that context, yearnings that were more toward the transcendence of God than toward divine immanence. Even then God was colored by images he had of his father, images formed by what he had been told.

As would be expected, there were some in our sample whose families never went to church, in whose homes there was no recollected mention of faith and no religious practices remembered. One layman said it for these: "Faith was just always there. I can't lay it on anyone. Now and then there was a pastor or a Sunday school teacher who helped a bit, as I began to go to church alone. But faith just seems to have always been there."

Many of the childhood homes represented in our study were economically poor. The childhood of our total sample was marked by the Great Depression. But at least for some, poverty seemed to deepen trust in a caring God, enriching the diversity we are illustrating. A professor of rich faith mused about his childhood home: "The whole understanding of life was from the agency of God. There was no need in our family that did not have at some point either an expression of gratitude to God that he had made something possible or a petition to God to make something possible. There was a profound sense in the family that there were not sufficient human resources to guarantee any outcome." During the Depression a son and his father shoveled snow. The mother interpreted the money earned as a result of God's work. "Because Mother saw God in it, I saw God in it." A sense of divine agency at work extended beyond bread and butter and dollars and cents. For example, a sister was ill with lobar pneumonia. Mustard plasters were applied. The mother called the family together in the living room and all prayed that God would spare her life. She recovered. Prayer got credit along with mustard plasters and poultices. A professor believed that maybe his faith began, consciously at least, when his mother gathered the family together to pray for his grandfather, who had had a stroke. "She showed us that she placed real value in prayer, and I think my faith began then."

Religion in these homes was not a one day a week affair. It was a part of the daily agenda. It related to food on the table and grades at school, to coping with illness and doing a job. It was real, earthy, personal. Life centered in God, whose will was the dominant factor in so many homes. The curious thing is that God and his will were not felt as frightening or particularly oppressive except in a few cases. God expected integrity, industry, and fair play. Parents gave evidence of trying to live by these divine expectations, which pretty much constituted their understanding of religion. There was little display or enactment of religion. One interviewee had a vivid memory of his farmer father frequently on his knees in his bedroom. A pastor recalled his grandfather reading his Dutch Bible. Gently shaking his head, the grandson said, "It all adds up to personal influences I can't unravel." But these memories were the exception. There was little remembered exercise of religion. It was just there: solid, rugged, not much talked about. Yet it pervaded the home and seemed about as natural as "brushing one's teeth," as one laughingly put it.

Yet most of our interviewees had somehow become aware as children that their parents' strength was fundamentally religious in its roots and its aims. This can be illustrated by how insight into forgiveness, so basic to the entire religious structure of our sample, was gained. The father of one of our people tried to teach God's forgiveness by pressing home the point that God does not hold grudges. What made the point for her was that she had received forgiveness from parents who did not hold grudges. She noted that her father's teaching held water, furthermore, because she had observed her parents as fallible and was aware that God forgave them. She gained a sense of security from knowing that forgiveness came from beyond the parents, from one to whom their lives pointed. A similar point was made by another: "I realized very early that there was somebody to whom my parents considered themselves answerable, as I had to consider myself answerable to my parents." Forgiveness that frees had come later for some of our subjects; but for most its beginnings seemed to be in powerful early impressions formed as they saw parents and other meaningful adults forgiving and forgiven. God became important to them because God was important to some significant adults around them, partly in the forgiving role.

Integrity within the home was the single most impressive trait to the large majority of our interviewees. They were impressed with the strength of commitment in their homes. What seems to have been so significant to childhood was that the home *stood for something*. It is noteworthy that while almost all of our subjects came to disagree with many of the beliefs of their parents, the fact of parental conviction was prominent in their memories. The homes were about evenly divided as to whether the mother or the father demonstrated strong convictions;

more often than not, it was both. (In a few homes grandparents dominated by their strength.)

In fact, in a few of these homes it was integrity, as valued by the parents, that kept the homes from involvement with the church and from religious practices. The churches were considered enemies of social justice, and religious commitments and practices were consequently devalued. Some of these fathers in these homes considered their labor unions more significant for achieving social justice than religious institutions.

The main reference for the strong convictions was usually God, but the commitments were to such diverse ends as hard work, frugality, truth-telling, respect for others, social justice, full employment of the mind, loyalty, sobriety, honesty, and dependability. One father was described as a Renaissance man who kept the family reading, thinking, and talking. Another father impressed his son with his honesty. "We children learned that you just don't lie over big things or little." A pastor whose father was a superintendent of schools acknowledged, "He wasn't my friend really, but I respected him highly. He resigned his job as superintendent when the Board cut the teachers' salaries. I remember driving out of town with tears in my eyes but proud of my father and the reason we were going." A son of migrant workers remembered his parents with deep respect and admiration. "They would make few promises, but when they did, as at Christmas, they *always* kept them." Our tapes contain in simple eloquence testimony after testimony to the integrity of parents. While mothers were women of equal integrity, it was the fathers who seemed to leave the lasting impression of dominant conviction. We have selected four samples of such testimony.

"Father was such a good person, a first-class human being."

"My father gave me the strength to go into adverse situations and stay with what I believe."

"He still represents for me the values of goodness, honesty, kindness. I want to be to my son what my dad was to me."

"I felt awe toward my father. He was solid and irrefutable."

These affirmations came from mature adults looking back from the advantage of distance and lifting up what was important to them. These did not appear to be compliments to deceased fathers, but simple statements of long-held perceptions.

What was impressive to people's childhood memories was that one or both parents had strong convictions and lived by them. This impression in turn helped to create in the mind of the child the sense that there was integrity in the home. Furthermore, the fact of commitment seems to have stamped the homes with the confidence that they were dependable. Parents to some meaningful extent lived out their commitments and gave out powerful expectations that the children should do likewise. For example, one man mused about his father's response to his trying to get out of doing a job on the farm because he didn't feel like it. "I don't care how you feel; the job's there to be done. If I only did what I felt like doing, I'd probably not gotten out of bed this morning." This straightforwardness, without double signals, marked most of these rather earthy homes.

Almost all of those interviewed said or implied that they had been raised to a strong sense of freedom and responsibility. We see a direct connection between this sense and the parental models who owned large commitments and personal accountability. The commitments were largely to a way of life that would be regarded as moral. God was seen in most homes as the primary sanction for morality. In the interviewees' childhood minds, God and morality were tied together, making for a powerful home ethos. We are suggesting that in the early tracings of childhood was etched the bench mark of integrity, and that integrity was somehow related to God, along with the concomitant values of freedom, responsibility, and dependability.

All of this sounds as if the homes were heavy on duty and light on love. The childhood and adolescence of most of our interviewees were lived through tough years: the Depression and World War II. Parental religious values were almost totally personal and individual. Hard work, individual responsibility, and a day by day seriousness seemed to be the dominant cast of most of the homes. Warm, tender feelings were not expressed easily. This is not to deny the presence of love, warmth, forgiveness, and the joys of families together. But it appears to us that feeling tones clustering around duty were dominant. It is significant that when warmth, love, and nurture were talked about, mothers came to the fore, as fathers had when strength and integrity were discussed. There were exceptions, but these were the patterns.

Most of our subjects felt affirmed in their homes, although sometimes the insight into such affirmations did not come until later in life, and now and then only through therapy. Occasionally childhood perceptions that a sibling was favored or that a parent's distance was a sign of no love seemed to block out signals of love. But the majority knew the continuity of love. The observation of one would stand for many: "Where the eros of me is, is in that family. I have no memory of alienation. We loved each other. We were just all together, and we knew it." Obviously, some families can express this love better than others. A woman got very clear signals from her mother that she had been incredibly happy that she and her twin sister were born. "That was an enormous message I'm really grateful for." At the other extreme is the professor whose mother was very reserved. "Strong affections were expressed through very small gestures. I had to read in a wink what I needed hugs and kisses to experience." We have to believe that in most of these homes there was a continuity of love, but the signals were not always clear. Children need an abundance of clear signals. We have to wonder if some of the parents themselves were not suffering from love deprivation and out of their own poverty of spirit could give only through the small gesture, or that they had had no models for communicating warmth and love. A few of our subjects indicated that they had come to this conclusion on the basis of adult reflection. In some cases, with the death of the father, a mother took on heroic proportions, as though released for greater expression. One mother, unsophisticated and retiring, coped well when the father died. She told the children that with God's grace she thought she could do what she needed to do. This was a sort of "coming out" event for her and seemingly created in the family a new spirit of togetherness. A pastor, whose Latin ghetto childhood experience had been bewildering to him and to which he reacted with hostility, expressed in a memorable sentence his gratitude for his mother after the death of his father: "I'm still under the warranty of her great devotion and sacrifice."

Love was sufficiently present in most of the homes to provide a sense of belonging and to form an analogue by which a child could initiate an appreciation for divine love. A younger pastor articulated very well the connecting link between love in the home and divine

The Return to Roots

love: "I saw in my parents a forgiveness and grace that made what they said about that even more real. God's forgiveness of us was not alien to what I grew up with. Mother was especially good with feelings, providing me with a reservoir of experience that supports God as active love in the world. The nurturing elements of God were transmitted through her. She helped with the formation of trust."

We are suggesting that there was a continuity of affirming love in most of these homes, some of it expressed clearly, some muted, and some becoming clearer after a traumatic event such as the death of a father. But in some homes it seemed partially buried under a value system of duty and obligation that loomed so large. Perhaps this very value system signaled to the children that you have to earn love by being honest, truthful, and responsible, a value system that gave way later, in some cases as late as mid-life, in favor of a love unearned, the grace of total acceptance.

In summary, affectional needs seem to have been supplied, abundantly in some cases, meagerly in others, but with a "continuity of sameness," to borrow from Erik Erikson, to form a nurturing matrix. Yet we are surprised that warmth and outgoing affection were not as paramount as we would have expected. Integrity, strength of character, and rugged dependability overshadowed the love potion. Caring elements seemed to yield to demanding elements, especially in the demands that parents put upon themselves. So parents became demanding role models for their children.

The climate permeating some homes was heavy with negation. In their religiosity these homes were purveyors of considerable guilt. One statement picks up on the level of guilt a number felt as they recollected their home environments: "As a child my faith was that God was loving; but be careful, be good, watch out, or he'll get you." Then he added, "I still believe in that kind of God, but he is softer now." Another put the same oppressive feeling less softly: "I had an inordinate load of guilt, in a fundamentalist setting. I was overly evangelized without a deeper sense of God's grace and acceptance in Christ. It came down to having to prove oneself. Religion was a thing you did. It was more extrinsic than intrinsic. The family helped instill a sense of guilt without relief." The theology of these homes placed on our subjects burdens of living up to a code. God was the ultimate enforcer of the code, with the parents his underlords.

Our picture is not complete without noting that a few other homes—perhaps 8 percent—were identified as pathological and were experienced with strong negative reactions. One mother made "everyone's life a living hell, but fortunately Father was a somewhat compensating factor." Another mother never let her children "inside her carefully defended, routinized existence." Her son said simply, "Mother always comes out gray." A father was perceived as domineering and manipulating. His son remembered from about nine years of age a Sunday school session. The lesson centered around the story of Joseph. "I remember thinking when the story was told, 'I wonder if the brothers know that he doesn't love them either.' That's what I felt. I was the favorite son, resented by my brothers, but never really felt Dad saw me as more than a star in his crown. What I did through my achievements enhanced his importance, but somehow I wasn't important in my own right to him. My whole drive to achieve was to demonstrate to my father that I was important." Another home was marked by the chronic depression of four grandparents and both parents. Several homes, labeled as religious, were centers of severe conflicts. Four used identical language to describe their homes as "filled with darkness." Yet children of these homes became women and men of faith, thanks to others in their childhoods or along the way.

The majority of those interviewed did not come out of their homes loaded with guilt. A few did carry that burden as well as other emotional scars into therapy in early and middle adulthood; most, however, emerged amazingly free of such encumbrances. We think the reason is the *quality of trust* that they experienced that their parents, or others in the home, had in God. One in his fifties could still remember his mother saying during a severe earthquake, "Yes, Lord, we hear you." Beyond the words he remembered no pleas, no begging, no bargaining, only a calm and calming response. Expectations of right and good pervaded the family structures. There was a quiet solidness about these expectations that our subjects appear to have internalized. We were impressed with the ego strength of all our subjects. It is our judgment that these strong egos as a group had their postnatal genesis in these familial contexts of integrity and strength. Perhaps integrity and strength were forms of love that children failed to identify as love. Nevertheless, most of our subjects felt sufficiently secure in homes marked by devotion to ideals and the resulting integrity that the homes were sensed as nurturing and supportive even if warmth was not a factor to which many called special attention.

While there is no single pattern of home life requisite for faith formation, the kind of home experience enjoyed by the vast majority of our subjects appears to be good soil for the growing of faith. That the home is of fundamental importance to childhood is an accepted fact; that it is of similar importance to faith formation is the witness of these men and women who began their spiritual autobiographies with the home.

The Church and Rootedness

The response to childhood church experiences was mixed. Many had no early church experience. They were into adolescence or college before this was picked up. Some were too rurally located to participate in church life; the homes of others were indifferent to, or antithetical to, the church; and Sunday school and church (the way they most often put it) bored yet others. One of several significant differences between the professionals in religion and the laypeople in our study emerged in early church experiences. At least half of the professionals had rich memories of early church experiences, whereas less than a quarter of the laypeople could share such memories. The difference cannot be laid to the professionals' coming out of clergy families, for that did not happen. Their childhood homes, however, were far more church oriented than were the homes of the laypeople. We wonder if that close early tie between home and church might have been a causal factor in the vocation the professionals chose. For certain professionals and laypeople something important seemed to be happening in the institutional church, although its concreteness was not always clear.

For only a few did the pastors of their early childhoods make much of an impression! It was Sunday school teachers who came in for the greatest credit, although some were turned off by them, especially by their rigidity. One precocious youngster, now a professor of New Testament, quit Sunday school at four! He found no stimulation. Another quit going to church at about twelve years of age because her Sunday school teacher was not open to questions and her minister was loud and frightening. This is the one who told us, "My faith has just always been there. I don't know why." It will come as no surprise that Sunday school teachers were not remembered for their teaching. A layman said very straightforwardly, "A large share of what I received as a child and as a youth relating to Christianity and the church had to be gotten over."

What was remembered about teachers was their kindness, their loving concern, their faithfulness. These traits totaled up in young minds to Christian character. It was a Sunday school teacher who figured out that one of our subjects needed glasses; as a result, the shape of his world and his grades in school changed. Another teacher in the junior department first raised the question of college for one whose family had no history of college, urging that "our talents are gifts to be developed and we have a responsibility to use them for others." She died the following summer of cancer. "These two events were extremely meaningful to me," he said. A laywoman reported, "I had a fantastic Sunday school teacher when I was in high school. That teacher was concerned about all of us kids and our families. That teacher really set it up. I think that's how and where it began to happen! You go along with preparatory stages; then comes along one like this teacher . . . and it happens. After that come times of recommitment." Some Sunday school teachers had spiritual depth that they transmitted not so much through their teaching as through their personhood. Because they took Christianity seriously, as evidenced in their faithfulness to their Sunday school task, so did at least some of their pupils.

For a very few, pastors were important in early faith development, as fatherly people who were kind. But for most, their pastors did not know who they were and did not treat them as "real people," for example, patting them on the head as they went out the door while addressing the "real people," the adults. A few resented that the mail from the church never included them, only their parents.

The church experience of childhood days was both negative and positive. Church splits over preachers, conflicts over doctrine, over-evangelization resulting in a nagging sense of guilt, rigid teachers, boring lessons, preachers who could not deal with intelligent questions, the refusal or inability of churches to accept black people, and monotonous worship were distinct, unpleasant memories. For many they created the negative side of an ambivalence toward the church. The other side of the ambivalence, however, and what so often tipped the scales toward very positive feelings, was the sense of the church as an extended family. The adults were seen as parental figures who exercised some controls, evidenced a lot of love and concern, encouraged our subjects to think of themselves as rather special, and communicated to them that they saw in them potential, especially as they approached adolescence. A laywoman told us of her mother's death when she was only seven. The church came to the rescue and made up her family. "My need was social as well as spiritual," she said. "Since the days when that church family sort of took mother's place, my loyalties have been to the church community." One person could still sense the warmth of the church's people as somehow symbolically represented by the warmth of the church's carpets. Another expressed her delight in Sunday as a "fun day with the whole church family present and active." The experience of a black pastor also lifts up the church as extended family. As a black child growing up in a white community, he was taken with his sister by a white neighbor to a white fundamentalist church. They were the only black people. The congregation was warm, open, and caring. Even after he dropped out of Sunday school in his early teens because there was not much happening for the youth, the congregation continued to sustain interest in him. "They didn't preach at me, but held me sensitized to religion and spiritual values. The bonds of friendship are still there. I'm still in touch with this congregation. It's like going home. Much of what I am today I owe to that Sunday school and that adult context." Finally, one who saw in the rage of his mother what he termed "moral darkness," a darkness that settled like a pall over the family, found in the church a haven. In his words, "I saw in the church the rational sanity and stability I didn't have at home when the family was disintegrating. It was the only force for sanity I could see. With love in the church but not at home, I've had reason to turn to the love of God and the Lord Jesus Christ." He was the only charismatic among the professionals.

The influence of the church, however positive, was not the primary influence in early faith formation in our study. The chief insight about early childhood experience for faith that we have derived from this study is that the home, not the church, is primary. For most of our sample, parents or significant others in the home were actively involved in the life of the church. Their church activities tied home and church together. While the church itself lent value to early formation, the clincher was the respected, loved parents' putting their imprimatur on the church. They did not do this from a distance; they left their mark on childhood through what they said by way of their active engagement in the life of the church. As one pastor proudly put it, "Father led the family to church." Parents seem to have given the church respect! Later the church had to win or lose respect on its own. The initial significance the church has is given symbolically by the parents (or other significant adults) who say by their actions that it is significant. Defined as significant, it is significant to the child. That rootage seems to be deep.

That the church is important to childhood is not new. *How* it is important, that is, by way of parental signaling, was one insight that came to us from this study. We conclude that the home is the most important rooting for faith and that the church is really grafted to that primary root system. In this way the home and church form a root system that is capable of providing some of the soul's need for rootedness, of which Simone Weil speaks: "To be rooted is perhaps the most important and least recognized need of the human."[1] To be rooted, and to be rooted deeply, is important for faith formation. Here the word "important" carries the meaning of lifelong, recurring value. The rootage we are talking about is systemic, that is, a root system for the total organism, continuing to be effective throughout the life history of a person.

The Need for Roots

A very sensitive interviewee, in musing about his background, shared the insight that "when the religious impulse seizes the imagination, it will be in terms of religious symbols of that person's birthright." The birthright, as far as faith formation is concerned, can be described in terms of basic trust. It is a deeply laid perspective, a profound intuition of what is important, memory traces and feeling tones that are indelible. It furnishes primitive images and symbols by which to begin the picturing of embryonic meaning. It begins the process by which a composite of ideals is formed to direct the functioning of life. Our friends began there, with some idealization to be sure, but mostly with a rather healthy poking around in the fires of their pasts. What we found was that those fires are still aglow with warmth.

The faith of most of these homes and churches reflected a period of relative quiet before the storms of the atomic age. The Christian way of viewing things seemed natural and unproblematic, compared with just a few decades later. In this climate, most of our people had internalized an unproblematic faith. Though they had gone through intense struggles since childhood, and almost all articulated their faith very differently from their childhood experiences, they still reached back to feelings and symbolizations consonant with those primary and elemental experiences. Two examples at far ends of the spectrum stand for a large number of others. One who never attended church until he was twenty, having had no early religious experience or faith language, approached matters quite secularly. In a profound way his life, as he acknowledged, is still going on from old times out of a secular orientation. "I've not completely renounced my past and immersed myself in the church. In the narrow sense, I'm not a religious person. I have not that history; I don't use conventional religious language simply because it was never a part of me." At the other end is a pastor, involved in a ghetto ministry, who still has the longing for the older emotional life. He yearns to express himself in the style of that vitality that he knew as a child. While he longs to go back, he does not. He really cannot, partly because it would be an inappropriate regression, and partly because his matured faith states its truth so differently. He characterized his religious moves as from "visions to Yale." The emotional tug of childhood "visions" is there, with which he is in touch daily, but Yale symbolizes all the good and important reasons why he cannot go back. Yet in keeping with the principle that we return to our birthright, he keeps going back to the fires set in his childhood to warm his heart and rekindle his passion. Both examples go back; one to his secular roots, the other to his Pentecostal roots.

Not only did our subjects go back to childhood beginnings to chart the routing of their faith; they kept connecting the present with those primitive beginnings. Now and again throughout the interview they would return to the wells from whence they drew water. They seemed to *need* to establish congruence between the past and the present. A yearning to return to early childhood experience, not to replicate such experience but to be in touch with it, was naggingly present. This did not come off as mere nostalgia. Rather, a sense of organismic wholeness seemed to require any present elaboration of religious intuition and impulse to incorporate the efficacy of roots still very much alive. While our subjects had moved far beyond childhood beginnings, they had not merely doggedly fought the old patterns but had included them in the larger reaches of their faith experience. Later novelty included the synthesis of earlier, much earlier, rootage. The following bit of sharing captures the point: "Where am I now? I am searching for a unity of spirituality and social passion in such a way that as a twentieth-century intellectual of sorts I can fully, freely, and passionately deliver myself to the mission of the church. I know what it is to feel the presence, the delight, and the joy of the living God from my roots. How to discover that in the context of what I now know to be the case scientifically, theologically, and philosophically is an important question. I tend to think of this as a new development and another stage in my faith, which might possibly enable me to build on the evangelical resources of my roots and at the same time enliven the liberal concerns I picked up in my later development. Maybe these can function as a higher synthesis of faith."

We have learned from Freud, Erikson, Piaget, and child development people, among others, how important the events of childhood are. Our subjects touched only the tip of the iceberg. What they were in touch with was the feeling tone with which they responded to the whole iceberg. What came out was distilled by way of consciousness, but they gave us clues as to what was deeply residual in them through the routing of their early lives. The pilgrimage of their faith was rooted in early experience. With new experience came precious increments, some in traumatic, dramatic ways. But they felt the need to tap the roots that began their faith and even now were helping to power it. This moved one professor to put the need for roots and the power of roots in these anguishing words: "The question I am raising with myself is, How in the world can I communicate the power, joy, freedom that finally emerged out of that life experience (home-church) when I don't communicate the same ethos to my kids that was communicated to me? What are they going to ride on? I can't talk to them as a fundamentalist. Liberal Christianity is a Christianity of good will and important social issues. And kids are enthusiastic with that. But what's going to empower them to keep moving when it gets tough? What are they going to hold on to?" The need for roots is part of the soul's search for faith.

People who care and can effectively evidence their caring are crucial to early faith formation. What constitutes caring people? It is a dangerous and a dubious enterprise, as Ernest Ligon discovered in the 1950s, to develop a set of traits that educational theory—or any other theory—might try to inculcate into people. We are not proposing to develop a list of traits of caring people; what constitutes them is both idiosyncratic and utterly diverse. But we did find, in about 95 percent of our people, three very powerful perceptions of the significant others of their childhoods, which in numerous glad testimonies they shared with us.

1. As children they experienced in the caring people around them *integrity*. Two other descriptive terms were used often in the same context: genuineness and sincerity. Parents, grandparents, aunts, uncles, Sunday school teachers, neighbors—they stood for something. Perhaps a quarter of the homes were not religious or not especially

religious. But their children experienced what they later came to name integrity. Often the integrity was of a moral rather than a spiritual nature. The integrity pattern was relatively simple, informed by a few strongly held values, such as hard work, fair dealings, honesty, and promise keeping. Later, children began to see connections with church, religion, and God, if these were there.

Integrity was evidenced in how these important adults met everyday life. They seemed to deal constructively with it, whether it involved poverty, sickness, a job to be done, death, a tornado, moving, simple pleasures, or an emotionally sick one in the home. They showed a capacity to adapt to change. But they lived in the midst of life's vicissitudes in a patterned way that was consistent, dependable, and supportive. The children as children felt themselves to be in a fairly safe and secure environment.

2. As children they also experienced commitment on the part of some adults. Another term our people used was loyalty. The integrity seemed to come in part, at least, out of some commitments parents and others made to something beyond themselves. Early on, and with some much later on, they related this commitment or loyalty to God. But in its very primitive and early forms the commitment was to values, for that is what grandparents and others most often talked about: honesty, neighborliness, thrift, fair play. Hierarchical commitments gradually emerged, basic moral and ethical values slowly pointing upward to religious values and finally to the ultimate Referent, God.

Integrity came to be seen as a response of these important people to Something or some Other. Something or Someone beyond them held them in a kind of bonding, and their integrity somehow came out of this bonding.

3. Respect was the third experience they shared with us. They did not talk about the self-respect that parents

had enjoyed, although that almost had to be there. Rather, they felt very keenly that Sunday school teachers, parents, and grandparents respected *them*. It is curious that only a few used the word "love." Perhaps they assumed that as being present. What they seemed to be impressed with was the fact that even though they were children, they were respected; that is, they were for the most part treated as little people with rights and with responsibility for exercising their freedom within very definite limitations. Caring seemed to come through strongly when parents, for example, would do some listening, maybe enter into a brief discussion with them, and make decisions, taking the child into consideration whenever possible. The children seemed to sense through being respected *as children* that they belonged. They were not aliens in the family.

Can the church program an increase among adults of integrity, commitment, and respect for the other? Probably not, if these become the goals or ends of programming, not even if these are penultimate goals beneath the ultimate goal: relating people to God through Jesus Christ. Integrity is an idea, a possibility, that slowly forms in a person. It becomes a subjective quality within one, a defining characteristic of one's life. The significant others who impressed our sample as children derived their integrity from the ways they put themselves together out of the givens of their lives, within the milieu of their day-by-day living.

We think the church can help create people of integrity, commitment, and respect for others in two fundamental ways.

1. The church can help people actualize themselves, assuming all the responsibility that inheres in self-actualization, by helping people understand that before God, with other people, in the midst of nature, each constitutes or creates herself or himself. *How* that

self-constituting or self-creating takes place determines whether one possesses such qualities as integrity, commitment, and respect.

Abraham Maslow makes self-actualization the zenith of his hierarchy of human needs: physiological needs, safety needs, love needs, self-esteem needs, and self-actualizing needs. Alfred North Whitehead, the philosopher, makes self-actualization the core of the process of becoming. A favorite term of his is *causa sui:* We create ourselves. Out of all that God, history, others, and nature offer to us, we must respond by forming ourselves. We finally put ourselves together out of all the givens of life. Whitehead sees self-actualizing as a part of the ontological structure, that is, a kernel of what it means to be and to be human. Responsibility, for Whitehead, comes out of the requirement laid upon us to respond to the givens of life. Emil Brunner, the theologian, writes that it is the human being's essential nature to answer, to respond, and to enter into dialogue, ultimately with God. Our answerability, our response-ability, becomes our responsibility to make decisions, to reply to, and to answer others, and especially God. *How* we answer constitutes what we are—sinners, people of integrity, faithful, faithless.

Integrity, commitment, and respect for others are all qualities we create out of our answering. In this sense we decide ourselves, create ourselves, actualize ourselves, define ourselves. We put it all together, for better or for worse. *How* we put ourselves together constitutes *what* we are. One of the main tasks of the church, it would seem, is to hold before us our nature as self-creative and responsible, and to encourage as rich and positive responses as possible, out of which should come the integrity, commitment, and respect for others that was demonstrated by so many of the significant others in the childhoods of our sample.

2. The second way the church can help constitute people with such defining qualities as integrity, commitment, and respect for others is through accentuating the positive which is the gospel—that is, the good news of acceptance as is, of unconditional forgiveness, of being made right by the grace of God.

If people can be helped deeply and genuinely to come to a *new consciousness* that they are new people, a fresh creation, already forgiven, accepted by God as they are in their naughty, bad, sinful state, those people have a new starting point. They may not straightway reach out for integrity, embrace all the right values (whatever they are), and start to respect others, but they have a new beginning out of which new forms of being, new ways of being in the world, are now possible to them. This moves beyond mere morality, beyond new legalisms and rituals, to a different set of aims or goals set by each. A new consciousness of God who forgives unconditionally, leading them forward, can be the impetus for a new response to that gracious Leading. Such movement has a chance slowly, perhaps imperceptibly for a while, with fits and starts to be sure, to establish in the self the attitudes and behaviors of integrity, commitment, and respect for others that were demonstrated by the caring people who early on helped to root the faith of our interviewees.

In the next chapter, we move from early childhood roots to more contemporary feeders of faith, still concentrating on the number one influence on faith: caring people.

NOTES

1. Simone Weil, *The Need for Roots,* tr. by Arthur Wills (New York: Putnam, 1952), p. 43.

CHAPTER • 4

Communal Encounters: Feeders of Faith in Adult Years

The primary communities of home and church had fed faith in the early formative years of our people. That people continue to be essential to faith formation in the adult years was a strong finding. Perhaps 95 percent of our sample viewed people as the most important route of grace. They experienced God's caring through other people's caring. A number would agree with the statement of a religious professional: "People have taught me love, from which I have extrapolated the *agape*-love of God." Encounters with people were a primary meeting place with God. While Buber's I-Thou was not specifically mentioned, his concept of the communal I-Thou, in which another Thou becomes present in the meeting of two or more people who are present to each other, would catch up the integral meaning of the human encounter for the growing of faith of our interviewees.

Our sample was made in the main of strong people who took from others (as well as gave to others) out of their strength. Part of their strength was their recognition of their needs, the acknowledgment of their weaknesses, their profound sense that they were not a finished sculpture. They knew they had much to give, and they were just as sure they had much to receive. In encounters with others their faith seemed to keep them open to the possibilities inherent in I-Thou relationships. We infer that faith played a decisive role in their openness, for so many saw God as serendipitous, surprising them in encounter after encounter. In the intersubjectivity of the human I and Thou, the divine Thou became known. Through another's caring came the deepening intuition of God's caring. Whether they experienced change subtly or precipitously, in looking back they sensed God's creativity at work. Brought to a redemptive turn by another human being, they judged that God was redemptively busy. In human dialogue they were aware, sometimes much later, of divine presence. Part of the excitement of their adult years was the expectation that in meeting another, yet Another would be present.

These people had no doubt that communal encounters supported, changed, and enriched their faith as undoubtedly they did the faith of others. But as to which communities this was most apt to take place in, the data are not nearly so clear. Perhaps the I-Thou encounters were so much a serendipitous grace-gift that to classify them beyond a memorable moment or a name gratefully remembered would be an impossibility. We probed into a few communities to see if they accounted for such encounters in any significant or ongoing way. The data are indecisive, though they contain some clues.

In the last chapter we made the observation that the professionals in our study came out of homes that seemed much more religiously oriented than did the homes of laypeople, although for both faith was rooted in their childhood homes. Now we observe that the laity were more indebted to experiences with caring people in their adult years than were the professionals. For the most part, the professionals did not say much about communal encounters that fed their faith beyond their seminary or graduate school years. For example, many specifically pointed out that congregational life per se did not particularly help their faith to grow, though the demands of congregations did. Those demands sent them scurrying for help! On the other hand, the laity found their faith corrected, inspired, fed, challenged, and sustained by all kinds of human encounters. The professionals seemed to be more solitary individuals in their adult faith journey, while the laity seemed to be more corporate. Nevertheless, the professionals as well as the laity pointed to certain people who had nudged their faith, if not motivated it immensely.

The Church as a Community of Faith

We begin this section with the professionals and the painful difference between their theology and their congregational experience. They were in total agreement that Christianity is a communal affair and that the church is the community bearing through history the grace-gifts of God. Not surprisingly, we found among them a great sense of history. One, borrowing from Schleiermacher, a watershed German theologian of the last century, made the point that "theology is the explication of self-understanding of a particular religious community, including the appropriation of its historical tradition right down to its roots." The events that give rise to that community therefore form the distinctive kind of faith from which that community lives. The events that continue to occur in that community, in its identity and diversity, feed and challenge faith's intentions and hard-won realizations. Even the language of faith is given in community: the community's worship has a cultic language, its belief formulates a theological language, its history has a language created in dialogue between faith and culture, its devotion has a prayer language. The person of faith lives out of some tradition, a tradition that has shaping power. The people of faith in our sample were self-confessedly shaped in the Lutheran, Reformed, and Wesleyan traditions. But those were important streams emptying into a much wider river of tradition. Each was a tributary of richness forming the mighty Amazon. When these people spoke of the church as community, as often as not they were thinking of the centuries of ecumenical input that was effectively a part of their lives in the present. Profoundly, they saw community in a linear dimension, continuing from the past into the present; they seemed emotionally as well as spiritually buoyed up by this treasury. They had a profound sense of history, and they owned it gratefully as their history.

The community stretching back through its rich heritage calls for a response empathic to that heritage, that is, a communal response. As one put it epigrammatically, "I don't believe in the Lord Jesus Christ. *We* do. If *we* don't, *I* don't." What these professionals in the faith were saying is that their faith is a communal affair, the roots of which are in a treasured tradition. One cannot be a Christian by himself or herself, removed from this rooting, without being like a cut flower on the way to the trash can.

There was agreement that the church, with all its faults, is a vehicle of faith, and that it is impossible for present day Christians to conceive of transmitting the Christian faith apart from this vehicle. One woman expressed the agreement this way: "We are witnesses to the Resurrection, and that is a communal witness. Out of a belief and a commitment to Jesus Christ, I do what I do, and that belief and commitment is a communal event." It is primarily in the corporate worship experience that the "communal event" takes hold, according to these witnesses. In its cultic acts the church should register itself as a vehicle of faith, even if in corporate worship it so often fails this role.

But the professionals sounded to us as though they were talking theologically instead of practically; that is, they were voicing a theory instead of sharing a praxis. What is not clear is whether the church as a contemporary community is much of a vehicle for their adult faith. Only thirteen pastors and six professors—barely a third of our sample—said anything positive about the congregation as a community of people feeding their adult faith. At times it seemed to us that there was a "should" implied about congregational life, that is, that the congregation as a community should be a vehicle for feeding and sustaining adult faith. But the "should" was accompanied by disappointment that it was not so. There was clarity that faith is always a communal event, that the powerful tradition should be borne along through corporate worship, that in childhood and youth the church is an important vehicle; but whether the local congregation as a community of faithful people actually feeds and enhances faith during adult years was not clear. At least it was not clear that it did so for most of our professionals, and if it did, there was no identifiable pattern of how it did it.

Painful encounters within congregational life helped to grow faith, as a number of pastors reported. Through these interfacings some of them saw indications of God's sustaining presence and were taught a new humility as well as a new capacity to trust God. Some congregations offered no support and were actually a drag on faith, but in their very negativity they called forth faith. For example, one pastor noted, "My people drive me toward God. I haven't experienced much grace from them but in ministering to their needs I've experienced confirmation [from God]. Even the aridness of the desert has made me grow up a lot."

On the other hand, some congregations had within them strong support systems. The gentle, firm souls in such congregations were strong influences for faith. They became a family bequeathing warmth, acceptance, and support, and in doing so they pointed to the source of their caring. Their own faith became a finger pointing beyond themselves. Some church people by the simple eloquence of their loving, by the humility of their own being, helped a few pastors by making Christ available to them. It was most often a small core group of people that became the basis of deepening trust, growing commitment, and expanding belief formation. This might be a Bible study group, a protest group lobbying for human justice, or an official board serving in the role of pastor to the pastor. Sometimes it was only one or two sensitive souls who quietly and unknowingly shaped the faith of their pastors. The whole commercial notion of quantity lost all significance in our study. A touch of the genuine other in the human encounter took on shaping importance.

Furthermore, for some pastors a few Christian communities—for example, a support group of fellow pastors—nurtured faith by being profoundly open. This openness provided the climate in which they as pastors could say honestly where they were with God and with their fellow humans. This climate increased their sensitivity and willingness to listen, gave them courage to wrestle with problems endemic to faith, and provided a sense of direction toward reconstruction of beliefs. As might be expected, pastors more often than professors seemed to be the beneficiaries of the openness of laypeople. A professor or two found sustenance for adult faith in a congregation. A few more found it in their seminary communities, although, as we shall see, those were sparse.

Evidently the church that lives between memory and

hope has the makings of becoming a nurturing fellowship feeding adult faith. Sometimes it is a nurturing society, or at least a cellular bit of it is. But much of the time, it appears to border on the demonic when its rich potential of heritage and grace is suffocated by its preoccupation with the works of the flesh: idolatry, enmities, strife, jealousies, wraths, factions, divisions, parties, envyings, and so on (Gal. 5:19ff.). Then it seems incapable of that I-Thou relationship in which both the neighborly other and the divine Other might be known. This seems to have been a disappointment of both pastors and professors.

Laypeople had a quite different story to share about congregational input into their faith. There was a pattern. It usually began with the minister and then moved to the congregation. A thirty-five-year-old man, a graduate in business administration, paid tribute to a pastor he had while in graduate school. "He was the first man I could point to and say, 'That man is leading a Christian life.' He appeared to me to be a totally selfless person. His instinct was to minister to the needs of another. He showed me the power of being a Christian. That pastor is still after all these years a very special person in my life. It was then that I began to view myself as possibly being a Christian. I made a commitment to surrender my life to Christ. That pastor showed it to be possible and to be worthwhile." He continued, "Now, years later, I am in a church of two hundred members who evidence a spirit of caring, support, genuine love, concern. Those people are not just another gathering. They are a special place. I believe it is God's Spirit moving among those people. They are open enough to let that happen. Something is going on I can't explain in any other way."

A salesman's wife had a nervous breakdown and was hospitalized. His son was abusing drugs. In desperation he turned to a pastor for counseling. The pastor helped him to look at himself without being judgmental. Then he started going to church; there it "felt good to be. They seemed to understand me, how I don't know. I felt I had been given a second chance, almost as though I was reborn. I can now understand myself more clearly, what I like and don't like about me. The church was a good place to turn; the pastor and others cared."

A laywoman in graduate school carried around a lot of guilt. "My picture of God was so tied up with my father that he seemed always ready to judge me. I lived under long and deep prohibitions. Well, in graduate school I found a pastor who was like a breath of fresh air. I was so excited. Under my breath I said, 'I trust you; you have impressed me with both your knowledge and your faith.' At that point he didn't affect my behavior, but he freed me from my literalistic and negative view of the Bible. He helped me to see that some of those stories were not what they seemed. So began my freedom. The leaders in that pastor's church were much like he was: open, caring, accepting of me. They were so different from my father. I wasn't home free yet, but I was on my way."

One laywoman shared with us a very daring and courageous move on the part of her pastor. From college days she had had "active, concerned, able pastors." But when she was about thirty-one she was in a church that was rapidly diminishing in size, and its demise was on the horizon. The pastor talked to her one day about her potential. He told her, "We must have vision; we must be willing to change our ways. I want to urge you to go to a church a couple of miles from here, you and your husband. There you will gain new perspectives. It will be broadening for you. Your faith can grow much better in that congregation." She told us, "He was looking down the road five years when his little congregation would be dead. He wanted a different experience for us. His wisdom and his vision helped me to grow, as did the people to whom he sent us. They were much like he was." She broke into tears at this point; they were tears of gratitude for the vision of that pastor and the dynamic congregation she and her husband joined. "The new challenges were a growing up for me. It was an exacting faith-time in my life. It was threatening, and I knew I had to grow."

While pastors did not mean much to laypeople in their childhood, they were extremely important in their later faith development. When a pastor was supplemented by a caring, accepting congregation, the pattern was usually efficacious for faith development.

Higher Education and Faith

All sixty of the professionals, as would be expected, were college and seminary or divinity school graduates. As we noted in chapter 1, 39 percent of the 150 laypeople were college graduates, and 21 percent more had additional graduate degrees. These figures mean that 90 laypeople attended college. But we could not find any significant difference between those who did and did not attend college, in terms of faith, except for those who went on to graduate school. Even for them, college and graduate school basically made only two differences: (1) their world was broadened some, but the broadening itself was rarely related to faith, at least in any conscious way; (2) college peers became for a half-dozen a supportive group. Going to college made no more essential difference to faith than not going to college!

For the professionals, college was synthesizing for a few, disappointing for a few, mind-boggling for several, and stretching for many. As with the laity, some stretching was the result of many sorts of courses, whether in the sciences or liberal arts. But courses in Bible and religion opened most of our interviewees' eyes, forcing a new look at the faith they brought to college. The college road became bumpy for some, as biblical scholarship tangled with early conceptions. For others college provoked anger at Sunday school teachers who they felt had loaded them down with a lot of things they had to divest themselves of later. But there is a paradox here, as one put it: "In some ways I'm still emotionally a fundamentalist, but intellectually I'm free." Others systematically studied biblical and theological material for the first time, and they simply enjoyed the enrichment that came by way of new meanings.

What courses in Bible and religion gave to these people was a new set of questions. While some Bible professors were a negative experience, turning students off by their pat answers, most introduced students for the first time to critical tools by which to look at religion. They gave them permission to direct questions to their past and helped them formulate the questions. The goal of these professors was to elevate the sublimity of the Bible precisely through freeing the Bible to be itself by looking at it historically and critically. To only a handful did faith require that the Bible remain a sacred enclave, off limits to tough-minded scrutiny. A professor or two—rarely more—was singled out for praise for opening faith to a larger and more challenging view of the Bible. This was about the sole gift of college to faith, as far as they were aware. Peers added very little, and the church appeared to play a minimal role as well.

We need to follow the professionals to their seminaries. For fifty-six of the sixty professionals, divinity school experience was rated from good to excellent, though not without some misgivings, to be sure.

What seminaries did best for faith formation was

provide the intellectual climate, the tools of scholarship, and some of the important questions for the structuring of a belief system. The struggle in seminary was the struggle for understanding. One put it for many: "My seminary gave me tools for study, which a seminary ought to give, and not answers. Many of the answers of those years I've gone beyond, but seminary taught me how to handle the materials. It made me not afraid to look at anything. Without seminary I would have been more naïve and less critical. Criticalness enhanced my faith."

What we found was that the seminaries and divinity schools were doing what they have been accused of doing by many laypeople and some clergy: focusing the powers of the mind on the content of faith. They were doing this with the approval and gratitude of almost all our interviewees. They were seen as intellectual centers designed for the critical, objective study of theological and religious data. They were not perceived as tearing down faith. They were perceived as structuring faith so that it would be more worthy. Some of those who were unhappy with their seminaries had as a major complaint that their experience was not critical and constructive.

Professors *were* the seminary and became models and sources of inspiration in the birth of new understandings of truth as part of new dimensions of faith. Gratitude was expressed for individual professors as well as faculties as a whole. As one pastor said, "In my seminary there were great men and great minds. The highest profiles of value were there. It was the most deepening influence of my life." Of still another seminary a pastor remarked, "The seminary professors could laugh at themselves. Their earthy theology punctured a lot of balloons." A high tribute was paid to one school: "It was great to be part of an impressive tradition. I felt I had to be somebody. It drew it out of me. I was into something large, something to live up to."

Given these testimonies of appreciation, it is understandable that some of our interviewees revisit their seminaries as though they are making a pilgrimage. As one put it for several, "I go back to seminary just to walk around; it is where I expect my ministry to continue to be strengthened."

A conclusion we have reached from this study is that with few exceptions the most important people in the faith formation of our professional sample, beyond early home life, were seminary professors. For a few it was the faculty as a group. But for the majority one person (or at the most two) was the significant other. As important as a few college teachers were in the faith journey of our sample, they could not match the conscious influence of seminary teachers. Perhaps one reason for this was the readiness of these soon-to-be-clergy for clergy models. In the seminaries they found them.

It is dangerous to try to profile such a faculty person. But extrapolating from what we were told, we feel secure in describing that person as academically competent and intellectually alive, sharing convictions with a quiet confidence and personal authority, and caring with a sensitivity that is able and willing to be empathic. These would seem to be engraced people who touched their students unforgettably. Some were intellectual giants, but not all. Some acknowledged giants were never mentioned. But whoever they were, they became models for faith. They permeated young adult lives and perdured there to be called forth ten to thirty years later with enthusiasm, gratitude, and almost reverence. It set our minds to wondering about the layperson who is deprived of these meaningful people, and wishing for them a faith experience with a giant of faith such as their professional sisters and brothers shared with us.

Our data on the seminaries' contribution to faith may inform one response to a current concern in theological education and in the churches that the seminaries be much more responsible for the forming of faith in students studying for ministry. We acknowledge that the seminary student body of the seventies and eighties is a different generation from our sample. But our study would not lead us to think that seminaries can make up for what homes and churches did not provide by way of trust and commitment. The responses of our interviewees suggest that the seminaries are prepared to aid trust and commitment to seek and find understanding. But those primary aspects of faith would seem to be basically formed elsewhere, mainly in home and church. The seminary experience did mature trust and deepen commitment among almost all of our subjects, but the maturing and deepening presupposed something already present. What was there was there deeply and enduringly. Some of our sample noted that in their seminaries worship was weak, devotional life was often non-existent, community in terms of spirituality was rather sad. But there were few complaints! They came to seminary with the stuff of faith, basically amorphous and jumbled, and submitted it to tough cognitive inquiry. Through dialogue with their heritage in the theological struggle to say what the heritage meant, their faith seemed to come together for the first time. The belief form of faith began to take shape in earnest in their theological education at the seminary level. Trust and commitment were now seeking understanding. Seminary education gave them the tools for investigating, led them along the paths of inquiry, and challenged them to appropriate intellectually that upon which their trust rested and toward which their commitments pointed. For them that was enough. Their gratitude to their mentors was eloquent. They did not expect the seminary to do what home and church had failed to do. They were glad for this further phase of faith development.

Adult Friendships

For a very few of our total sample have adult friendships added much of which they were conscious. In a couple of cases, friends in military service helped by seeming to have a sure faith, which provoked a struggle: what's deficient in my faith? Out of this struggle a nuclear physicist has become a lay preacher. In that role he finds his faith growing in his contacts with clergy in the larger church.

In the midst of a family tragedy, a woman felt "helpless, guilty, impotent in my faith." She went to a meeting of women who seemed to have what she didn't have. With these women, meeting around the Bible, she felt new freedom, new power. "Perhaps I came to know Jesus really for the first time," she told us.

The fireman we shall meet again in chapter 5 joined a Bible study with fellow firemen, out of which came a "warm, close fellowship that I don't feel in church." Supported by this group, he rediscovered his early Baptist background and his "zeal to witness" became intense.

But most of our total sample evidenced a deep wanting for an intimate group, or a close other, to further their journey. One woman said she was no longer interested in "just keeping the machinery working. I want to go on a journey of my own. I'm tired of activities that mask the Reality. Sometimes we assume activities and the Reality are the same. I'm tired of words that don't seem to be productive. I think I need a small, intimate group to help me in my present need of self-discovery in the Presence of that Reality."

Only two laypeople commented positively on their business associates and their faith development. Most shrugged off the question, as though they had never expected any help from that source.

The professionals revealed a rather profound pathos when they talked about colleagues in ministry or adult friends, as far as their faith was concerned. They observed that much talk among colleagues centered around organization and ecclesiastical politics and sometimes professional theologizing, but rarely where one stands with God. Colleagues seem not to put themselves on the line. Professional peers evidently find it difficult to talk about themselves as religious people. For some this was a deep hurt. It appeared ironic to a few that in their experience the professional colleagues who knew the most about religious matters and who had invested so much of their lives in concerns of faith were not able to fulfill God's purpose to establish a society that would include matters of the heart as well as of the mind. One offered his explanation: "To avoid simplemindedness and the nauseating exhibitionism that so often accompanies the sharing of faith, colleagues have eschewed talking about where they are with God. In those few cases where it does happen, it seems to be one of those marvelous happenings."

On the other hand, some colleagues have been helpful in the shaping of faith. A staff assistant prodded his senior pastor, whose training was solely in classical terms, to rethink his theology in terms of where people are and where their values are. The senior pastor began to trust his own experience more. As a result a congregant noted to him, "I am sensing with you no final answers but a struggle, and it makes me want to struggle." A black man had a "Timothy-Paul" relationship with a slightly older black pastor, who was his first powerful black role model. This older colleague "introduced me existentially to grace," he said. "He set grace free in my experience and liberated me. I found out there was far more to the relationship between God and his children than I had ever known. I came to see God as Father and Friend instead of that cold, judging, rigid God I came out of Bible school with."

In studying and sharing with groups of pastors, some have found stimulation, nurture, and validation of themselves as people of faith. Said one, "I would be high, dry, and diminished without that ecumenical group of pastors." Then he added, "I wish laypeople could have this kind of experience. It would both strengthen them and also change them." Through both single colleagues and groups of peers, static and stale faith has been rejuvenated, and some have felt that they were helped to experience God at more effective levels

What seemed to set a few colleagues off from others was the quality of their being. A woman put it this way: "Some you admire, some you don't. You admire those who show human capacity and concern, care, integrity." "Genuineness" came across as a key descriptive word. Colleagues who personify a quality of life make their faith so appealing that they become models for faith formation, though they themselves are unconscious of the modeling they do. It is as though some colleagues, perhaps diverse in beliefs, have a quality of spirit that blows upon the souls of those about them and inspires them to some higher ground. But these choice spirits seemed to be few in number. Deep hunger aches for intimate sharing within the dimensions of faith, which surely would enrich the personhood of the professional. So many expressed gratitude for the interview that allowed them to say where they are in faith, as though the need for intimate sharing waited for a right moment. We felt strongly that professionals sharing with professionals at faith levels would enhance faith and might be productive of richer ministry.

Contemporary Family Relationships

Although we had to ask very few lead-in questions, we usually had to raise the question of whether the contemporary family affected faith. In many instances the question came as something of a surprise. Several said when the question about the spouse's influence was raised, "That's an interesting question," as though they had not thought of a wife or husband feeding their faith. This occasioned one of the longer pauses in the interviews.

With regard to spouses not much of substance was forthcoming, with a few exceptions. The word "supportive" was the key word. One man said, "My wife and I support each other at an intuitive level. A lot of our faith has been unsaid." While most couples seemed to have basic congruence in matters of faith, evidently they talked together very little about their faith. A wife's faith did help to keep one man faithful to what he professed. "I knew what she stood for and what she expected of me." The example of what a pastor's wife endured without a word of complaint in living in the inner city was a never-ending surprise and inspiration to her husband's faith. With joy in his face he said simply, "At home I'm comfortable. She is strength for the growing of my faith." Another paid tribute to his wife as being the "major mentor in my faith development. She is a naturalist who uses no God-language and is instrumental in forcing me to rethink and rearticulate my position." A woman shared, "My husband is my clue to Christ. His acceptance of me was the clue to Christ's acceptance of me. He proved himself as trustworthy; so I could begin to see God as trustworthy." Yet the fascinating turn of events is that her husband was not a church-goer. After her conversion he began to attend church because he had seen her change. In two cases, clergy husbands learned from their wives total love. In each case they learned what it is to be cared for in an "unfaltering way," having confidence in love "so secure, so total, that nothing could take this away." Such love not only shaped their personhood but gave them empirical clues to the total way God cares.

Our impression is that not more than one-fourth of our 210 people saw their spouses as intrinsic to faith development. The rest either were not aware that there had been any influence or felt that there had not been any in an important sense. Couples evidently talked little about their faith. Their own faith did not become agenda for sharing. The exceptions delighted in such sharing; the majority were taken aback by the question, as though it was startlingly new.

Children were a different story. While they did not appear to affect the faith, consciously at least, of at least a half, they did a number of things to the faith of the other half.

They broadened it. Children have turned out agnostics, skeptics, and unchurched, as well as committed believers either in the mold of their parents or doing a new thing. Offspring have taught their parents that faith also finds expression outside traditional formulations and institutions, a teaching that these parents had known, of course, but now more existentially. There was pain in the recounting of where their children were and what they were doing or were not doing with their faith. But the pain had been, or was being, absorbed in the faith-stream of these parents. Parental faith stretched to include patterns of belief and worship that at times seemed alien. Thus, children opened vistas that forced rethinking and new acceptances.

Children challenged faith. They did this in a number of ways. Their difficult questions prompted probings and responses, which in turn reshaped faith. A child of four saved some money to give to the poor. Evidently this prompted him to reflect, and he asked his mother, "If God is their Father, why doesn't he feed them?" Another asked his mother, "Why does God make that one die?"

Parents were educated by their children to be honest with them, to struggle with the straightforward questions children ask. Children were prods against flat, simplistic statements.

So children turned out to be liberators. Sometimes this was a psychological liberation. Children helped several to see things about their own childhoods they had missed by being on the receiving end of the parent-child relationship. These found faith itself opening to new levels of trust, as old blockages gave way when children occasioned the replay of old tapes. New psychological understandings liberated faith to be more adventuresome. One man turned to his own parents and in a flood of tears became partly a new person, as he shared in intimate ways what he had been longing to do for years. Little children had led him. Parenthood also made faith more public. As one said, "Marriage and fatherhood almost brought my faith out of the closet. They liberated my faith, for they forced the lessons of faith to be practiced at home, the only complete home experience I ever had." A professor, musing in an existential mood, questioned his practice of faith at home, the question most raised by the parents as they thought about their children: "Have I been loving enough? Have I let my faith control me? Or have I bracketed my faith and acted as an individual by myself as under no aegis of God? Do my children see that my faith makes a difference?"

Children posed to faith the problem, How do parents open up the Christian faith to them? Because most of our sample had a robust respect for freedom, including the freedom of children, many rejected imposing on children either their religious practices or their ideas. Some read the Bible at mealtime and some said prayers with children. They went to church with them. They intended to be examples, with what rigor and discipline they could muster. They would try to communicate about love, respect, and justice. They wanted it to be known to their children where they were in trust and commitment. But they did not want to impose their "religion" on the children. A layman said it for many: "I am concerned that my children grow up in a more open spirit than I did." Some felt guilty about not doing more. But they did not know what more to do within the family structure than to try to be present to their children so that faith could take hold of the children as it had taken hold of their parents. Many were concerned with the question of how to have a vital faith in the second generation. As a female professor asked, "I know my faith is mine; my parents didn't make it mine. How then do I help my children to know their own faith? My horror is to raise three nominal Christians, because my faith has been so exciting through the years." It seemed to us that we were listening to faith in one of its finest moments: anguishing but trusting a providential Caring to use whatever they might drop into the family milieu to effect faith in their children as that Caring had effected faith in them.

This problem did open their eyes anew, if they had been closed, to what the church was trying to do. Their children helped to validate the significance of the church community. One put it so well: "My family has given me greater appreciation of the church, because I sensed how powerless as an individual I am to make an adequate religious contribution to my children. It increased my sense of dependence on the larger community." He continued, "Not knowing precisely what to believe and teach regarding changing values accentuated my need for other people to help." Another put it this way: "My husband and I have tried to analyze why we have remained Christian. It is largely because of growing up in a Christian community with a sense of identification with that community. So we have worked hard to involve our children in the life of the church community and to help them understand what their baptism means." They and others discovered that family and church must work together, each supporting the other, with a new consciousness that the family and the church together are inculcators and renewers of faith.

Finally, the contemporary family experience, particularly the children, furnished analogues to faith. Especially did the concept of grace as unqualified acceptance become more deeply meaningful. As a pastor noted, "My children have taught me beyond anything else unmerited love. I can be an awful person at times, and the next day they've forgotten about it. It's a new day and I'm their father and they love me and I love them. Theological forgiveness has become existentially meaningful to me partly because of my experience of being accepted by my children." Another had seen more deeply into the fatherhood of God from siring and fathering two daughters. The very concept of God changed for one man as he and his son grew together. They had been fiercely competitive. The father was forced by the son to give up controlling him and to let him go. He slowly came to the confidence that he could trust his son. He told us that his son's coming of age was important to his own coming of age. "I was shaped in this relationship. It was important to my theological development. I could no longer accept a concept of God which involved him as above and detached, an unprocessive understanding of God. Increasingly, an incarnational understanding became important." Not all or even many were this philosophical or theological regarding the impact of children on faith. But most were taught by their children, and their Christian faith was illumined. These were for the most part sensitive people, able to learn from a little child. Their agenda of faith was life, and the child enlarged the agenda.

CHAPTER · 5

The Bible: Almost Closed

If our sample is at all representative of the church as a whole, then the Bible, despite its holy and authoritative aura, is virtually closed. That will not come as a shattering piece of news even to casual observers of the religious scene in the United States.[1] A continuing complaint of pastors is the biblical illiteracy of their people. And yet the churches' educational offerings in Bible find only the same few opting for them.[2] At the same time most Christians, including those who do not read the Bible, would agree that the Scriptures are basic to their faith. One can start a fight very quickly by denying the inspiration or authority of Scripture, even among those who never read it.

Historically, the Bible has occupied a place of preeminence, at least with its leadership and in its creeds. The story of God's covenantal dealings with wayward humanity, the Bible depicts the many faces of grace, culminating in the portrait of Jesus of Nazareth and fulfillment through him of the long-promised salvation events. The written Word gives testimony and shape to the living Word, the Christ of God. As the unique and authoritative record of God's gift of new life, of God's requirements for that new life, and of God's promise to fulfill ultimately what God has so graciously begun, the Bible is the source book of the good news.

But This Is What They Said

Half of our lay sample had to be asked about the role of the Bible in their faith journeys. Half of these, while acknowledging the Bible as basic, candidly admitted that they do nothing with it. The other half read the Bible (Southern Baptists were the most numerous in this group), but most of these use only a very small part, and that often irregularly. (The Sermon on the Mount is first choice.) Of those who read the Bible, half do so literally. A third of the literalists were college graduates, while only 2 percent of those who had gone on to graduate school were literalists. We found no difference between those who had graduated from college and those who had never attended college as to who did or did not read the Bible. Those who attended graduate school read it least.

From that half of the laypeople who do read the Bible with some regularity, we learned a few things. Not surprisingly, many of them read it in "fits and starts," as one man described his reading. He continued, "Even my best resolve doesn't get me to Scripture. I fall into bed or prefer to read something else." The "fits and starts" approach to reading the Bible seems to be connected with a crisis in one's life. A Vietnam war veteran started to read the Bible when he was faced for the first time with his mortality. In the midst of the dead and dying, he began to question the whole meaning of his life and "who or what was controlling it. I was voracious in my study; it included a systematic reading of the Bible and church history. I was searching for meaning." An engineer who described his faith as "very operational" reads often from Corinthians, Romans, and the Sermon on the Mount, for there he finds the Bible applicable; that is,

The Bible: Almost Closed

it meets his life where he is living it and where he needs direction in "operational terms" to help him cope with day-by-day living. He finds no blueprint, nor is he looking for one; that would be too enclosing for him. Rather, he gains a sense of direction from Paul or from the collection of kingdom requirements Jesus set forth throughout his ministry. But most of those who read the Bible, whether with some regularity or in "fits and starts," are looking for specific answers to their day-by-day problems. The literalist interpretation fits these people. As one said, "The Bible is a sort of recipe book."

Inner yearnings fueled some with desire to read the Bible. A Southern Baptist woman just "loved to deal with ideas." She turned to the Harvard Classics and to the Bible. She said she had a "hunger needing to be satiated." A university administrator was seized with the question, What would it mean to take Christianity seriously? To answer that question he began to struggle with Bonhoeffer, Tillich, and the Bible, in that order. He concluded that to take Christianity seriously would be the most revolutionary notion possible. This has become a controlling idea for him. "Actions have to square with the biblical portrait of Jesus, and Bonhoeffer's choice and sufferings made the light of Christ shine through." Thus he came to his compelling vision. Running through the various motivations for reading Scripture was the aspiration for inspiration. It was as though at least some were trying to reach beyond themselves for a larger identity, and fitfully they turned to the Bible with some expectancy that in its pages their aspiration could be met.

Those teaching in the church school had their own motivation. One such teacher said, "There must be a growing edge. The Bible furnishes that. It is constantly taking on different dimensions. I am seeing richer perspectives all the time. This is necessary for my teaching the adult class." A woman committed herself to the Bethel Bible curriculum to prepare better to teach. She knew she needed to grow in understanding, the better to communicate her faith as a church school teacher. About a third of our sample who read the Bible claimed they did so to sustain or grow their faith.

An interesting comparison develops when we look at what the professionals in religion do with the Bible. Out of sixty only eight set time apart to read the Bible for the good of their own souls, quite apart from their professional activities. Nine others acknowledged that they read it with this intention very erratically. Proportionately fewer professors and pastors read the Bible for personal growth than did laypeople. Most of the professionals did not even mention the Bible with regard to their faith formation. The reason, we think, is rather obvious: vocation and faith for them were inextricably tied together. They sensed that their professional work was continually forming their faith.

All sixty of the professionals use the Bible almost daily, and some for considerable periods of time. In the process of preparing sermons, lectures, Bible studies, worship services, and so on, they are in and out of the Bible. Thus, these professionals have a built-in advantage over their lay brothers and sisters, whose preoccupations are in the world of business, labor, politics, homemaking, or professions. The laypeople have to move from the work world, which is basically secular, to a few moments of private worship or Bible study. That move is difficult, and it takes a deep motivation. Admittedly, the Bible is a strange world for the modern layperson.

On the other hand, our professionals were constantly working with the Bible. They did not have to find time for or make room for it. Some did evidence a twinge of guilt for not having set times for Bible reading, but we surmise that this may have been an overhang from an earlier piety, or that they were urging their people to do something they were not themselves doing. But any guilt did not seem particularly burdensome. We are not concluding that their faith would not be richer if they had some more scheduled occasions of a retreat-like nature. We are accounting for their minimal structuring of personal devotional occasions around Scripture precisely because of their heavy vocational involvement with the Bible. While they did not specify a particular role for the Bible, it is at the base of much of what they do professionally.

The laity, on the other hand, not vocationally involved in Bible study for worship, preaching, or teaching, are not daily immersed in the Scriptures. The professionals have the decided advantage. What they do vocationally, the laity at best does avocationally. Relatively few laypeople do it, and do it with zest.

Recognizing the Bible as an "absolute requirement for Christian faith," one professor proceeded to tie its use to his professional work. "It interlaces my theological teaching and writing." For another, his teaching in church history "is not even conceivable apart from relating historical themes back to the Scriptures." In sermon preparation the pastor turns to the Bible as his or her source book, in the process of which biblical metaphors, such as the wilderness wanderings, the Exile, and the potter and his wheel, help to tell the grace story, and exegetical work opens up fresh, relevatory insight.

The impressive point is that the Scriptures used *vocationally* affect the faith of the user. A professor has put it very succinctly. "My professional work in New Testament has a very profound effect on who I am and what I want to do with my life." Another New Testament scholar said, "The continuous study of the Bible does feed my faith. I think there is an openness to whatever

Scripture might say for my personal faith and my participation in the body of Christ. My radical treatment of Scripture is within the context of prayer and love for Scripture to free it to be 'itself.' " A pastor told us he was certain that people's faith would be enriched if they had to prepare a sermon regularly, implying, of course, that his faith had been so enhanced. These illustrations are not isolated. They are representative of some of the professionals in our study who, with exceptions, use critical tools of scholarship for the purpose of letting the Scriptures "be themselves" so that God can use them in the divine grace-work. In the process of working with the Scriptures, they find themselves to be recipients of that grace-work. While professors may deal more critically with the historical material as a professional function, both they and pastors alike grow in faith out of the involvement. (It is not particularly significant, but it is interesting, that proportionately more professors than pastors spelled out the place of the Bible in their faith development.) There is a personal appropriation within the intellectual, exegetical inquiry. One pastor put it this way: "All of a sudden I as a workman become the workman addressed. All of a sudden I've heard my bell. It's become the Word." In a similar vein another confessed, "I, too, have responded to it, as when the good Samaritan becomes an ethical directive for me."

The Bible is nuclear to the faith experience of these people, but is so enmeshed with their professional lives that half did not single it out for special treatment. When they were pressed they said, "Why, of course"—and many said little more. There is a little doubt that the Bible figures prominently in their faith formation, but we are wondering if it would were they not professionals. The laypeople have to move from the world that preoccupies them occupationally to the strange world of the Scriptures. Can the churches provide stronger motivation than they are now doing to encourage the layperson to make this move?

Three Proposals

One temptation is to be freewheeling in making suggestions about how to make the Bible a much more open book for the laity. But we can resist that temptation, since laypeople themselves have provided clues about recovering the Bible as a major means of grace. The first two proposals are explicitly theirs, and the third proposal is at least implicitly from them.

Small Group Bible Study

There is no question as far as this study is concerned that caring people are the most important factor in faith formation, as we have seen in chapter 4. Many of the people in the sample said that the Bible became most meaningful to them in small groups. The first proposal brings together caring people and small group Bible study. (This does not apply to the professionals who did not mention group Bible study as important to their own growth. Their vocational work motivated them to do independent study.) We interviewed two firemen who with five other firemen worked twenty-four-hour shifts. This meant dormitory living. One of the two interviewed had proposed that they study the Bible together in some of their spare time. The response ran from some eagerness to mild reluctance, but the seven did agree to try it. Bible study was the focus of the group at first. But gradually two foci developed: the Bible and supportive fellowship. As we listened to the second fireman, who had been a nominal American Baptist, it became difficult to tell which was the more important, the Bible or the group. The Bible took on tremendous meaning for him in the context of the group. His faith was literally born anew as the group gradually developed into a rich, supportive fellowship, which it had not been before the Bible study began. It was as though the Bible gradually began to shape the group, and the group began to form itself in each other. The second fireman came alive religiously neither through the Bible alone nor the group alone but through the two together.

While, of course, the details differ, several laypeople spoke of the importance of Bible study within the nexus of a group of some sort, whether neighborhood, work, military, college, or church. A friend invited one woman to a Bible study in her home. "All of a sudden the Bible started opening up. I went for a year. It was life-changing." Socializing, coffee, the Bible, caring support—she specified these aspects of this significant experience. Contextually, the Bible came alive. Now she reads the Bible "a lot" alone. Now she teaches it in a nursing home. Now she is struggling for theological understanding of such questions as, Why do the righteous suffer? How can a good God do this? It all began when the Bible was opened up in a group in which she felt cared about and cared for.

A nurse joined a nurses' Christian fellowship, through which she "got into the Bible." There she came to understand it. The group and the Bible taught her to pray as she worked with cancer patients, "Help me, Lord, to get through this day and get through it the best I can." Through those days, traumatic for her in the midst of suffering, she found strength in the constellation of group, Bible, and prayer—listed in her order. She had been in other groups. She had tried to read the Bible alone. A fortunate group experience that included the Bible seemed to her the right mix. A war veteran almost echoed the nurse's story. Only the theater differed: a Bible study in a group of scared but supportive men near the front lines. Together they "reconstructed the Gospels" as their own lives were being "reconstructed along faith lines." In the midst of this he came to a visceral conclusion: "I knew there was a God; I knew I was being looked after."

But not just any group makes the Bible come alive. Sometimes the church school class did, but most often it did not. It was often a head trip, and a poor one at that. The presentation was usually a lecture that only revisited old material. And in much of the adult educational program there was no saving feature, such as a genuine sharing of insights or feelings. Odd as it may sound, people seemed to be hesitant in church in expressing an honest opinion that differed from the party line. That hesitancy seemed often to hold people back from sharing problems and expressing genuine fellow feelings.

They did not say it in so many words, but we began to wonder to what extent the right group could be planned. There was something serendipitous about those Bible studies in the firehall, the home, the nurses' dorm, on the battlefield. We sensed some irony in the possibility that the church's educational program was not always the richest place for Bible study! There were classes, and some information got transmitted. But the Bible rarely seemed to become a catalyst for rearranging life, for honestly sharing in an accepting environment. People in the class were caring but in the class itself Bible study seemed not to be in touch with people, with their needs, their questions, their doubts. Bible study in a typical church school class was a study *about*, not a meeting *with*. There seemed to be a latent understanding that the Bible was set, certainly in text but also in interpretation, and free discussion was not often encouraged. Permission to question, to doubt, to advance a different idea seems not to have been granted. Not all experiences of church school classes were this way, of course. But the most vigorous and invigorating Bible studies that were recounted by our sample took place outside the church.

Does the very church building suggest such an official and authoritative structure of thought and practice that within its walls the Bible cannot become the catalytic agent that frees people to be as honestly and genuinely themselves as possible? Is there Sunday-go-to-meeting posturing, precisely because of the holy day, the holy place, the holy atmosphere, that militates against the kind of sharing often done outside the church? We are not pointing to, or even suggesting, radical departures from traditional interpretations of Scripture. Probably in most cases there would be no departure at all. What we are concerned with is an obvious contrast between Bible studies in a church and those outside. The contrast consists primarily of a feeling content. Bible studies outside the church seemed to provide an atmosphere of acceptance where people felt relatively free to express themselves, including both negative and positive feelings and thoughts, whereas within the church, and more especially Bible classes, there was a party line and if one deviated very much he or she would be suspect.

Our findings support at least in part the position taken by John Westerhoff III in his *Will Our Children Have Faith?* Religious education requires a socializing context. Needed is an "environment that supports the expansion of faith"[3] and not its encirclement. In such a communal context, Bible study seems to have a chance to come alive and to become a means for the growing of faith. This should not be at all surprising. The Bible is a very communal book. It comes out of a community (the Old Testament out of Israel, the New out of the early church). It is the communicated, shared complex of the memories of a community. In turn, the Bible helps to create community, as the Exodus material did Israel and as the entire Bible has helped to shape the Christian church.

The Bible: Almost Closed

The proper context for its use is communal, for that is its unique nature, as James Smart has shown.[4] The Bible is witness to, and interpretation of, the mighty acts of God in covenantal relationship to communities of people. It stands to reason that a social milieu is appropriate to further witness and interpretation, as the laypeople in our study have related.

But can the churches be that environment? Perhaps they can be and sometimes they are. But the churches may ironically put too many strictures on the Bible, taming it, playing it too safe and proper even though their gospel is high-risk stuff.

Part of the difficulty of the typical church school seems to be methodological. Lectures *per se* were not eschewed by people in our study. But the lecture method so often elicits little holistic response. What our people seemed to be telling us was that the Bible came alive and they grew only when they got caught up by Scripture in the company of others also caught up, and when honest sharing took place. There seemed to be a yearning to grapple, but not alone, and to grapple without many limitations imposed. It wasn't that they wanted to be heretical; it was that they wanted to feel free to say how Scripture was meeting them and how they were responding. In the midst of an accepting, caring group, the Bible's story seems to have a better chance to become their story. Sara Little makes the point so well, as she quotes a student after a group Bible study: "I cannot remember when my mind has been so actively engaged as when we were probing Bible passages and commentaries and quotations in our exploration tonight of the term 'the people of God.' But then when I suddenly realized that we in this room *are* 'the people of God' as we listen to one another, care for one another, are bound together by a common purpose bigger than any of us—*that* moment was when I *knew* what the term meant."[5] (Sara Little's book contains excellent group interaction models for teaching and learning.)

But in the midst of all this there was a reservation and a complaint.

Pastors as Teachers

The laypeople were very hesitant even to sound like they were criticizing their pastors, past or present. But gentle criticism there was, and a few times it was very forceful, that their pastors did not do enough teaching, especially of the Bible, and that when they did teach, too many of them seemed to be rehashing old stuff. A few paid tribute to the teaching ability and the content of their pastors' teaching. A Lutheran said his pastor was a better teacher than preacher because the pastor's teaching provoked his interest more and sent him home thinking.

Now we are on shaky ground. We feel secure in making the judgment that the vast majority of our laypeople were traditionalists. They were scarcely thinking of higher or even lower criticism of the Bible. At least a quarter were literalists. We suspect, for example, that few if any knew that there are two creation accounts in Genesis, hundreds of years apart. And yet some seemed to be sensing that there was much more to the Bible than they knew. A few complained that they felt cheated. There was a history they did not know, a history within the Bible as well as of the Bible. There were interpretations that were nebulous to them but that they sensed would help in the understanding of Scripture. They wanted to know more. They knew the Book was holy, but they did not have it within themselves to say why. One woman, an American Baptist, got into a "demanding Bible study, almost like a college-level course. I loved it," she said. "Up to that time Bible study had not been demanding. It had been a pooling of generalities, a mutual sharing of opinions but lacking in depth." Through the demanding Bible study, her faith grew. "It was grounded now in the Word. Now I had the feeling I knew what I was talking about. It gave me a lot of freedom."

Pastors were seen by laypeople as the trained persons in their midst. They had been to seminary (a very unclear kind of school to most). They wanted them to share with them their encounters with and journey through the Scriptures. They did not eschew lecturing. But they wanted their pastors to share their struggles with the Bible, out of which had come hard-won positions, and they wanted this sharing in an environment of acceptance. They regretted, and a few resented, that pastors taught very little, that they often taught warmed-over stuff, and that they taught too often in an authoritarian manner. The laypeople respected pastoral authority; they did not appreciate its misuse.

We came out of the study wondering what theological seminaries had done in their Christian education courses, wondering about the role models provided by professors, and wondering why the content of seminary Bible courses had not been appropriately shared with the congregations the graduates served. Are pastors afraid of what they know, afraid to share that with their people? We thought we heard a yearning for truth.

Would first-rate teaching by the educated and trained professional in the congregation—the pastor—and first-rate content help make the Bible come alive? If so, perhaps the importance of the Bible would not have to be urged and argued but would become obvious, as the Bible was allowed to become the unique and authoritative Word. Is the Bible too protected to be itself? That is, do some theologies of Scripture become barriers against Scripture? There is and must be a doctrine of Scripture. But how that doctrine is understood by laypeople may prejudice their wrestling with the Bible. To some it seems a hands-off book, one they have to be very careful about lest they err against it. They are often reticent to say what they think and how they feel about Scripture. After all, it's a holy book! Perhaps this is a major reason why there seems too often to be no meeting at more than a superficial level between the Bible and people. Both the Book and the person would seem to have to be free (relatively, of course) for a meeting to take place between the I of the person and the Thou of the Bible.

This requires competent teaching and an atmosphere of genuine acceptance. The pastor is an authority. That is both the clergy's strength and weakness. Strength, because pastors can give permission to honestly look at the Bible, out of human need, and to confront it even as it confronts the person. Weakness, because pastors can use this authority to enforce their way of reading it, not allowing, much less encouraging, free exegesis under the Spirit of God, and not encouraging lay readers to grapple with texts even though their backgrounds and perspectives may be quite limited. If the pastor can be content with mini-lectures to open up a passage, and can at times confess his or her questions, confusions, and problems with a passage, that pastor might provide both the acceptance and the model for the layperson's own dynamic engagement with the Bible. That kind of permission might grant the necessary freedom for a people-Bible dialogue to occur. One well-educated layman made this very point. A relatively new pastor conducted an eight-week, midweek Bible study. Evidently with some care, he pointed to and illustrated various forms of biblical material: poetry, historical narrative, preaching, myth, stories. He also pointed to historical accounts that were in disagreement. He tried to show what the author might be trying to get across in a particular passage. Said the layman to us: "You know, that freed me. I always felt I had to apologize for the

Bible. I knew it was important, but sometimes the way it sounded embarrassed me in a Bible class. It didn't make sense. It was so foreign to my human experience. Yet I felt I needed to defend it, embarrassed though I was. When the pastor opened up the Bible, I knew I didn't have to park my brain. The Bible became a new book to me."

The Bible and Preaching

In the chapter on the sermon we note the low estate of that communicative event. We were not told by our interviewees that there ought to be more careful expository preaching. But we have wondered, Do preachers need to open up the Bible more intentionally in the chief worship service? That is when they have the largest gathering of the congregation. That might well be the targeted time for a deeper educational thrust to preaching. If our people were among the most faithful in their congregations, and if many of them scarcely read the Bible, perhaps a concentrated attack needs to be launched from the pulpit to counter the gross biblical illiteracy in the churches. We are far from proposing a biblicism that would only rob Christ of his central place and continue the churches in their woodenness, and that would be untrue to the Bible itself, which is a record of and a witness to the mighty acts of God. Nor are we countenancing any withdrawal of the church from its prophetic stance toward injustices in contemporary society. On the contrary, biblical literacy is an enemy of injustice. A thorough knowledge of the prophets, Jesus, and the apostles would underscore God's demand for justice. Getting into the Bible is not getting out of the world. A careful reading, study, and understanding of Scripture disturbs the conscience and calls one as a servant into the world where God is at work among the dispossessed, the hungry, the hurting, the sinful.

This is not the place nor are we competent to make a lengthy homiletical statement on expository preaching. But we do know that such preaching can be, and often is, deadly; then it is a libel on a very exciting book. When preaching is irrelevant to life, then the Book about the abundant life is being grossly misused. When preaching consists of a set of moralisms, then the dynamics of the Book are missed. Preaching is sometimes only paraphrasing, or more typically, eisegesis (reading into the Bible pet theories and biases), whereas it ought to be exegesis. If preaching does not translate into "marching orders" for the week, as Karl Barth has remarked, it is not the Word alive with God's Spirit.

The professionals in our study who spend hours each week carefully studying the Bible for preaching and teaching know that they must translate what the Word has said to them for their congregations and students. The excitement in the pastor's study is part of the dynamic of expository preaching. Insights gained through critical biblical research during the week, when shared from the pulpit with a congregation that has not had the training, the motivation, or the opportunity to do the research, can encourage the dialogue between modern persons in the pew, laboring to understand God in their times, and men and women of the Bible, who labored to understand God in their times. Every congregation pays the preacher for this, to be crass, and has a right to expect biblical competence and professional workmanship to appear in the pulpit Sunday mornings.

A pastor made at least part of the point we are trying to make about expository preaching when he talked of preparation time: "Study and research for sermon—making impacts my life as the struggles, failures, and accomplishments of the biblical personages make me take a second look at what it means to be a person of faith." The rest of the point is that sharing that study and research with the pilgrims in front of him on Sunday morning should impact their faith journeys as those journeys become the location and the moment for good biblical teaching. This might also raise the status of the sermon, which so often uses a text in the most superficial way possible: as a point of departure into what is essentially a topical sermon, for which little biblical grappling has been done.

Good expository preaching is very demanding; for starters, it requires a number of hours a week in careful scholarly work. The congregation should demand it, as the preacher should demand it of himself or herself. And the congregation should also assure its preacher the time for the disciplined study required for research and exposition. Then perhaps one of the benchmarks for identifying the church, as articulated by John Calvin, will reemerge: the right preaching and hearing of the Word.

NOTES

1. James D. Smart, certainly no casual observer, has agonized over the "growing silence of the Scriptures." See *The Strange Silence of the Bible in the Church* (Philadelphia: Westminster, 1970).

2. In a doctor of ministry research project, Philip E. Perkins offered ninety-eight people various options for study in the church school. Fourteen opted for the Bible and eighty-four indicated they would rather deal with other material. "Establishing Sharing Group Programs in a Parish of the Episcopal Church" (D. Min. diss., Pittsburgh Theological Seminary Library, 1977).

3. John H. Westerhoff III, *Will Our Children Have Faith?* (New York: Seabury, 1976), p. 50.

4. Smart, *The Strange Silence,* pp. 23ff.

5. Sara Little, *To Set One's Heart* (Atlanta: John Knox, 1983), p. 51.

CHAPTER · 6

Prayer: Number Two But Narrow

Prayer is a perplexing subject in this study. It ranks number two, second only to caring people, among the factors making for faith. It is the most important factor at the adult level in the growing and deepening of faith. Yet very few of our 210 laypeople and professionals said why or how it is important. The professionals, on the whole, were no more articulate than their lay brothers and sisters about what prayer actually did to or for their faith.

About the same percentage of professionals—52 percent—claimed prayer as they did the Bible as a major means of faith. But they did not engage in prayer, as they did in Bible study, primarily as a function of their professional life. Prayer was for them what it was for the laypeople: a devotional activity meeting the needs of their spiritual life. Yet the percentage of about half is misleading. That percentage refers to pastors and professors who talked of prayer as prayers said or spoken not as part of their professional duties. A number of others claimed for prayer a central place but had in mind not articulated prayers but the soul's being present to God in a more constant spiritual posturing. Many of the professionals who acknowledged prayer to be foundational to their lives expressed disappointment that articulated prayer was rather haphazard, a "from time to time experience," largely undisciplined.

For 79 percent of the laity, prayer was claimed as crucial to their spiritual well-being: sustaining faith and promoting growth, times of guiding, cleansing, healing, and renewing. Some (15 percent) found prayer ritualistic and somewhat static. For only 6 percent did it have no personal meaning. The laity were inclined to understand prayer more in the sense of prayers said, although a few, like their professional counterparts, also sensed that prayer had much to do with their being "before the Lord" in unarticulated ways.

What we think we learned is that prayer is a "surrounding climate," as a pastor put it. That is, sometimes prayer is a distinct and separate act, to which reference was made as a "now and then thing," but fundamentally prayer seemed to be viewed more as a constant response of the self to the Reality that surrounds, permeates, and informs the existence of the self. It is as if prayer is a conforming response to the incursions of grace, whether grace is imagined as an act or a flow, and not a series of set times, though such times brought the more habitual response back into consciousness. Perhaps prayer seen this way explains the basic inability of our interviewees to distinguish prayer for meditation. Some had used Zen, for example, as a method to detach from things so as to focus attention on the divine Reality with the intention of developing a habit of the soul. Our interviewees seemed to be pointing to the profounder level at which prayer was conceived. Thus prayer appears to denote a relationship of response, central to the religious life, which sometimes is lifted up into a momentary act of consciousness called "a prayer." Though these "prayers" might be said often through the day, and though some of our sample might have twinges of guilt for not engaging in more of these momentary "prayers," the real struggle we sensed was to effect the response to the Divine as a constant undercurrent of one's whole, answering life.

Prayer—articulated and unarticulated—was without doubt the *sine qua non* of the religious life for our sample. If we can extrapolate from our interviews the essence of what it is to be religious, it is to pray. Prayer is the building of the inner world. It is the source of spiritual strength and power that defines the inner reality. It is more than introspection, more than words, more than agendas. It directs one's life in total response to the God of the Gospels. Now and then—perhaps many times a day—this directionality of the soul voices itself in words. That is a prayer act catching up a deeper movement of the soul as a stream of response to God. We are not suggesting that the stream always stays within its banks. It goes awry into ditches, losing its true aim. But prayer seems to have much to do with the soul's intentionality, with aiming and re-aiming toward the Reality where the soul's home is. One of our responders stated it this way: "Prayer is the attempt to submit ourselves to the God of the gospel out of the perspective of the gospel. For instance, intercession articulates the way we perceive ourselves and others not in an everyday perspective but from the perspective of the gospel."

Prayer is the total involvement—feelings and commitment as well as words and gestures—of the religious self. It is part of any Christian (or religious) existence. One put it in the form of a confessional: "This is who I am, Lord. These are the things I like and don't like about me. In doing that I build on grace. You don't say who you are to anybody but to one whom you hope or believe will accept you, at least at some level. The deeper you get, the more you build on grace."

We have noted the play back and forth between conscious, momentary communications between the self and God, on the one hand, and the deeper level of directionality on the other. Our sample would be embarrassed by any suggestion that they had attained this deeper level. But we think that is what they fundamentally meant by prayer and that the means or acts of prayers were eruptions from the depths. Yet acts should in no way be minimized. One found posture important, being on her knees in quiet and peace. Another eschewed group prayers, while some found groups enhanced the meaning of prayer. A charismatic prays in tongues when "I can't think of anything else to pray. Maybe I don't know what to pray. In speaking in tongues," he continued, "you put your mind in neutral, essentially, and just let the nonsense words flow. You have to trust the supernatural presence of God, letting him work through you. It's part of the reality of God's presence." To one whose theological struggles were of crisis dimensions and who came through the long crisis with a new sense of reality, prayer as activity is still puzzling. His candor is refreshing: "Sometimes I pray in ways that fit the sense of reality I had as a child and don't really fit the sense of reality I have now, and sometimes in ways that are integral to my present life. Prayer has become a function of something else, more than being the centrally shaping, nurturing activity when I was a child, that is, a more self-conscious activity based on reflection. Does it make sense to pray, and if it does, what is the form that does make sense? And if I believe that it does make sense, why am I not doing it more often? I am very much impressed with the power of prayer. Much of my internalization of family faith was through prayer; it was a shaping factor and as a child as natural to pray to God as to talk to my parents. It was a deep part of my existence." He expressed disappointment that he does not pray as often as he senses he should. Yet in him we sensed dramatically the two emphases we have been making: prayer is a form of his being that erupts on occasion in a conscious, articulated act.

Both professionals and laity had profound insights into both the nature and meaning of prayer. They acknowledged, sometimes gladly, the significance of prayer in the faith journey. Yet in interview after interview, especially with the laity but also with the professionals, we thought we heard the echoes of a distant cry, "Lord, teach us to pray." One of the few criticisms laypeople directed toward the pastors of their adolescent and adult years was their failure to instruct them in how to pray. They were acutely sensitive to the crucial role prayer plays and so they felt deeply that they ought to have been helped to pray. They faulted their pastors for assuming that prayer just comes naturally. They were embarrassingly aware that so much of their prayers was " 'Gimme' stuff" and superficial thanksgiving, that is, thanks for the obvious and the commonplace. It was as though they were searching for greater authenticity in their prayers, perhaps like the disciples heard in the prayers of Jesus to his Father, prayers that must have seemed so different from their own and from those they heard other rabbis praying.

From the pulpit, in classes, and in one to one encounters, pastors have rich opportunities to upgrade the prayer life of their people. If prayer is number two in the growing of faith, and yet those who pray feel their prayer life could be greatly enriched, pastors would do well to consider making a major effort to teach contemporary disciples how to pray. Of course, what our professionals told us about their prayer life might suggest that the pastors themselves may feel the urge to echo the request of long ago, "Lord, teach us to pray."

It is risky in a few pages to try to set forth the ingredients of prayer. Yet it is incumbent upon us who are recommending pastors do some basic teaching in prayer to suggest at least some direction. Our interviewees dealt a bit with confession, mostly of weaknesses and sin, with thanksgiving, and with petition, primarily centering around personal and family needs. Every pastor has on his or her library shelves a book or two fleshing out the nature and practice of prayer. Nevertheless, we are suggesting the acronym, ACTS of Prayer (despite a deep suspicion of acronyms because of their often mechanistic nature and superficiality). Prayer is an activity of the soul nuclear to faith, which needs some analysis. The acronym, ACTS of prayer, gives us a handle on a very perplexing activity:

> **A**doration
> **C**onfession
> **T**hanksgiving
> **S**upplication[1]

A few of our interviewees, professional and lay, in sharing insights with us have suggested some of the ingredients in the ACTS of prayer.

Adoration

A pastor reflected: "Prayer is a celebration of the Presence. It may be short in time duration, made up of specific moments of thanksgiving, confession, intercession. At bottom it is organismic celebration." A layman also talked in terms of Presence: "You can't separate any of life's activities from that Presence. All day long we are making responses to God. We are keeping in touch whether we are consciously aware of it or not." A Baptist woman said it almost with a sigh of joy: "I guess my favorite subject is prayer. I can't seem to get away from praise and gratitude in my prayers. I feel so richly blessed." "Praise" was the primary word used by interviewees to describe the response of adoration of God.

Briefly we shall try to focus on the meaning of adoration as far as prayer is concerned, borrowing from six significant sources. In an old book on the doctrine of prayer, James Hastings wrote, "Adoration is the homage of the creature to the creator. . . . In such adoration we bring our soul into the ineffable light of God's presence; we do not seek actively to understand Him, but passively we let our soul lie in His sight."[2] One of the giants of devotional literature, Saint Frances de Sales, writing in the seventeenth century, talked of adoration in terms of aspiration: "Make frequent aspirations to God . . . by short but ardent movements of your heart; admire His beauty . . . ; adore His goodness . . . ; fix your interior eyes upon His sweetness."[3] An even older classic is *The Cloud of Unknowing*, dating back to the fourteenth century. The unknown author advises, "Lift up your heart to God with humble love: and mean God himself, and not what you get out of him. . . . A naked intention directed to God, and himself alone, is wholly sufficient." Such intention is the "sharp dart of longing love"[4] that is at the core of adoration. Much less known is John B. Magee's fine study on prayer. He writes: "The practice of adoration—looking to God in and for Himself, losing oneself in His majesty and the beauty of His holiness—sets religion in its proper and saving focus." And he adds, "The practice of adoration also gives depth to all the other moods of prayer."[5] Paul Tillich has the church in mind when he writes of adoration, but his words apply as well to private prayer. "Adoration . . . is the ecstatic acknowledgment of the divine holiness and the infinite distance of Him who at the same time is present in the Spiritual Presence."[6] Tillich goes on to show that adoration includes the contrast between the creaturely smallness of the human being and the infinite greatness of the Creator, but at the same time includes the participation of the one adoring him who is adored.

Finally, we turn to Thomas Merton, who lingered long over "prayer of the heart," as he called it, and shared his reflections with us. "By 'prayer of the heart' we seek God himself present with depths of our being and meet him there by invoking the name of Jesus in faith, wonder and love. . . . The climate of this prayer is . . . one of awareness, gratitude, and a totally obedient love which seeks nothing but to please God."[7] A new kind of self-awareness emerges, a self-awareness *in the Presence of God:* not isolated, alienated, or narcissistically oriented. "Prayer. . . means yearning for the simple presence of God, for a personal understanding of his word, for knowledge of his will and for capacity to hear and obey him."[8] To summarize our quick journey into the thought of these who have reflected so deeply on prayer: adoration is the soul's deep intention to focus itself in love on God and to participate in that One whose Presence creates the ultimate environment for the life of the soul. Adoration, therefore, is the first and primal activity in the life of prayer. It seemed to us that this is what many of our 210 interviewees were asking for in the cry that we thought we heard out of the depths, "Lord, teach us to pray."

Confession

After claiming prayer to be the second highest priority in their faith formation, only a few, as we have already noted, ventured to describe the content of their prayers.

About one in ten talked about confession, for example. Those who did saw confessional prayer as a time of cleansing, healing, and renewing the self. We have to assume that if prayer is as important as our interviewees claimed, confession plays a much larger role than they thought to acknowledge. Whatever the unsaid role of confession, probably it can be deepened to make that activity of prayer a profound means of growing faith, and as a corollary, of growing a new self.

If we take the appropriate petition in the Lord's Prayer, "Forgive us our debts (or trespasses), as we forgive our debtors (or those who trespass against us)," we are profoundly into the nature of confession. To begin with, in confession we are making a statement about who we are: sinners. Confession is cheapened when it deals with mere moralisms. Then it is cheap confession, doodling about the edges of our existence. Confession in the biblical sense is always about sin, and sin is always defined *before or in the presence of* God. Therefore, in confession the confessor is saying who he or she is before the Lord: not only one who adores the Lord but one who at least compromises his or her adoration. Confession needs to follow adoration because we are essentially double-dealing creatures: in aspiration we yearn for the very Being of God and in sin we turn away from God to go our self-directed ways. The statement the confessor makes totally exposes him or her before God. It is an organismic confession; that is, the total person, from within outward, says who he or she is. The psychological value is that the *whole person*—body (*basar*), heart (*lev*), soul (*nephesh*), to use biblical analysis—is integrated in a unifying confession of sin, analogous to the unifying confession of adoration.

But the question immediately arises: can we accept forgiveness? The answer seems so simple, so sure; of course, isn't that what we want? But do we? For forgiveness comes at some cost. If we are honest and holistic in our confession, it means we are intending to form a new self as our grateful response to the forgiving God. But we truly love the old self, even though it is more a love-hate we have for the old self. Can I tolerate a changing identity, let alone embrace it? Genuine confession—and anything less is a hypocritical statement by the self—implies I want a radical transformation of the old me. That is the theological doctrine of repentance. So confession is a costly venture.

But, finally, confession raises the question of whether I can endure the responsibility of forgiving my debtors and those who trespass against me. That onerous proviso that Jesus inserted, akin to loving the enemy, is part and parcel of confession. If I ask for forgiveness, I take on the responsibility to let the flow of forgiving grace from God course through me to right a wronged relationship between another and myself.

Our interviewees said prayer was very important to their faith development. Confession as a statement the self makes about itself and its yearning to be transformed says in part why prayer is so important.

Thanksgiving

For almost all of our people, prayer was a small or large celebration, a "Thank you!" Here is the locus of one of their two primary emphases in prayer. They were grateful to God, and daily they told the Lord so. They were thankful "for every breath," for "things physical and non-physical," "for an oak tree, its beauty, its structure, its endurance," "for the recovery of a loved one from illness," and so on. Our interviewees seemed to be celebrating in a thankful way their God and the divine goodness and generosity. We wonder if adoration and a clearer understanding of confession might even enlarge the horizons of this thanksgiving?

Supplication

The act of supplicating is humbly to present an earnest petition for self or others to God. Supplication needs to be seen from two perspectives: for self and for others.

For Self

After thanksgiving, the most common petition in our study was for self, family, and, with the laity, for the pastor. We lump these under the heading of "Self" because family and pastor represent primary communities, the most intimate concerns of the self.

These prayers often reflected the simple concerns of everyday life: "Help me to find my lost keys," prays a biblical scholar of international renown, a prayer he labeled a probable compulsion, aware that God would not take him by the hand and lead him to his keys, and yet aware that God might quiet his anxiety so that he might regain his wits and find them. A laywoman prayed that God would help the plumber find the shut-off valve. "God even cares about pipes," she said. "Why not?" Another laywoman prays that the "Lord will help me find bargains, or at least more significant ways of spending our money." Yet another laywoman put her prayer needs at a quite different level. "God and I seem to be involved in something I'm living out in this life. I'm part of a larger purpose God has. I'm supposed to play some part in that overall scheme of things. Prayers of my seeking a ministry: my way of trying to say to God, 'What would you have me to do?'" But one layperson said it was difficult for her to pray during a crisis. She reflected, "Maybe I have a problem in constructing an appropriate prayer. Maybe there's a reluctance in me to say, 'Thy will be done' in time of crisis. Maybe I'm afraid of what might come; maybe I can't trust God with the consequences. And maybe I must be in control."

What supplication for self, family, pastor, and sometimes neighbor seems to mean to professionals and laity alike is twofold: (1) prayer for specific needs and wants and (2) prayer for more general needs: to be sustained, for strength to live from day to day, for guidance, for patience and understanding, to be healed, to be renewed, with the prayer for strength paramount. This seems to suggest that most of our interviewees did not feel the need to beg God to take over their responsibilities. Rather, they wanted God to empower them to do what they needed to do or ought to do. They did not come off as though they were under a "tyranny of the shoulds," to borrow from Karen Horney, but they did come off as a responsible people supplicating the Lord to strengthen them to fulfill their responsibilities.

For Others

By "others" we mean the world beyond the family and close friends, the "world out there" of widows and orphans, of poverty and hunger, or warring factions and nations, of crime and prisons, of racial and ethnic discrimination, of politics and economics, of environmental balances. With regard to this world we noted one of the great differences between the professionals and the laity. As a whole, the professionals made regular supplication for the world in all its need. As a whole, the laity did not. There is some tie between the two groups' interceding or not interceding for the world and their different ethical concerns for the world, which we will discuss in chapter 9.

What our study indicates is that laypeople need a great deal of teaching and encouragement to pray intercessorily for the world. The evening television newscasts, as well as newspapers and news magazines, supply the agendas for intercessory prayer. But the laity need to be warned not to try to lift the whole world to God. Sensitivity to a part enables one to pray more thoughtfully. The more one gets acquainted with a part of the world—for example, the Middle East, Central America, northern Ireland, South Africa—the better one is prepared and motivated to let his or her soul bear the cost of lifting that part of the world to God. One should not tell God what to do. That is not the function of prayer. But an informed person of faith presents to God the passion of his or her soul in behalf of the hungry, or the war-ravaged, or the tortured, leaving that passion with God to use in God's struggle to create a more just world for all. Such supplication should have a powerful impact on a believer's ethical and moral stance toward the world in its need, a problematical area as we shall see in chapter 9.

We close this chapter on prayer with a statement from that biblical scholar who prays for help to find his lost keys. Convinced that extraordinary things do occur, he has difficulty in urging God to change the divine mind, as in the case of illness. Yet he makes impulsive responses. He turns very naturally to prayer when he is anxious about anything. But prayer is never an effort to convince God to do something other than what God is going to do. Through all the revealed inconsistencies, he saw the basic characteristic of his prayers to be "simply trust. My prayers are the response of trust: I can trust God. I know with my mind that there's much about prayer that doesn't make any sense at all, but with my heart I still pray. I have learned to live with the paradox. I guess I don't want to dissect a living thing."

NOTES

1. James Hastings, among others, lists these activities within prayer. We have rearranged his topics to fit the acronym, combining petition and intercession under supplication. James Hastings, *The Christian Doctrine of Prayer* (New York: Scribner's, 1915), p. 47.
2. Ibid., pp. 48, 63.
3. Francis de Sales, *An Introduction to the Devout Life,* tr. by John K. Ryan (New York: Harper, 1950), p. 56.
4. *The Cloud of Unknowing,* tr. by Clifton Walters (England: Penguin, 1961), pp. 53, 61, 68.
5. John B. Magee, *Reality and Prayer* (Nashville: Abingdon, 1957), pp. 52, 53.
6. Paul Tillich, *Systematic Theology,* vol. 3 (Chicago: University of Chicago Press, 1963), pp. 190, 191.
7. Thomas Merton, *Contemplative Prayer* (New York: Doubleday, Image, 1971), pp. 30, 31, 33.
8. Ibid., p. 67.

CHAPTER · 7

The Sacraments: What's Wrong?

Our study can be most faulted in its depiction of the relation of the sacraments to faith, because it intentionally excluded the entire Catholic tradition, which is essentially sacramental. Had the Episcopalians, for example, been included in the study, we might expect a somewhat different set of findings on the sacraments. Of course, that expectation might not bear up. Our expectations had been that the sacraments would be significant in the forming of faith within the six denominations, Reformed in origins as they are; for the Reformation placed great emphasis on the sacraments. They were one of the marks of the church for Calvin, when rightly administered and received, and they were signs of divine favor and Real Presence among God's people for Luther.

But the sacraments did not fare well as means of grace or as occasions of grace among the majority of both professionals and laity, in our study. In almost every interview we had to inquire about their role in the forming of faith. In this chapter we shall note what little our interviewees shared with us about baptism and the Eucharist, and with each of the sacraments make some suggestions that might make faith more aware of these two means of grace, of the values potential in them but apparently not realized in any conscious way by many.

Baptism

When we inquired about baptism, six professionals said it had some importance and four others said it was significant in their continuing faith. But they did not say how it was significant. One quarter of the laity said it was symbolically important or mystically important. If it had not been for American Baptists and Baptists, the figures would have plummeted. For example, 80 percent of Presbyterians said nothing about it even when asked. And 60 percent of Lutherans said nothing or that it was not important. What saved the Lutherans in some small way was that a few years prior to our interviews the Lutheran Church in America had studied baptism in their adult Christian education series, and a few of our interviewees referred to this study—some evidence for the value of adult church education![1]

The World Council of Churches' Faith and Order paper *Baptism, Eucharist and Ministry* says:

Baptism initiates the reality of the new life given in the midst of the present world. It gives participation in the community of the Holy Spirit. It is a sign of the Kingdom of God and of the life of the world to come. Through the gifts of faith, hope and love, baptism has a dynamic which embraces the whole of life, extends to all nations, and anticipates the day when every tongue will confess that Jesus Christ is Lord to the glory of God the Father.[2]

This statement on baptism, as with the statements on Eucharist and ministry, was fifty years in the making. This gives us a strong clue as to how significant ecumenical leaders consider baptism to be. The verbs express the power of baptism: initiates, gives participation, embraces, extends, anticipates. Baptism is a faith-laden event. Yet relatively few of our sample made anything of it. Some of those who did saw it profoundly, as did a Lutheran pastor who had been struggling with his own identity and who theologized about baptism within that struggle: "It's an each day experience, for each day I must decide who I am going to be. Am I going to act out my baptismal covenant and identity or become somebody else?"

A fellow Lutheran found in the continuing acts of baptism fresh reminders of grace. He described these acts as "grace-loaded. In baptism God publicly claims us, gives us a name, and makes us his children. That's its theology. The question for me is not how do I get right with God, but how do I experience all that he has given me? Not how am I to be born again, but how am I to live this life God has given me? How am I to live out the birthright God has given?" For a few professionals every baptismal service was a time to take inventory of their faith. They put it in personal terms: my identity is with Christ. That's what my baptism means. Am I living out faithfully that identity? Not a single layperson and only a few professionals said anything about baptismal identity or how baptism related to their faith, when the question of that sacrament was raised. Our study provided no indication that Lutherans could say with Martin Luther when besieged by doubts, anxieties, guilt, fears of failure, "I am baptized." Because Luther believed that it is God's Word (Christ the Word) that constitutes the sacrament, and that baptism is God's promise to release us from the tyrants—sin, death, the devil—through our participation in dying and rising with Christ, Luther needed no other affirmation than "I am baptized." No counting of new birth experiences for Luther. He saw all of life as a "daily baptism, once begun and daily continued."[3]

Whether it is recovery of old meanings for some or

new knowledge for others, the continuing meaning of baptism evidently needs to be stressed. The World Council paper *Baptism, Eucharist and Ministry* proposes two ways to underscore the meaning of baptism.

First, in the context of each baptismal service, scriptural images and teachings that inform baptism should be presented. The paper lists these elements as central to the theology of baptism: participation in Christ's death and Resurrection, conversion, pardoning and cleansing (water), the gift of the Spirit, incorporation into the body of Christ, and the sign of the kingdom.[4] Since the act of baptizing may be fairly lengthy, this would be a suitable place for a mini-sermon, as suggested in chapter 8, pinpointing only one of the aspects of baptism noted above. The refrain that might run through many baptismal services, connecting them over a long duration, would be that baptism is the work of God. While sometime it must be appropriated in faith, and it requires daily reappropriation, decisively it is God's saying, "You are mine. I accept you as you are unconditionally. My grace is sufficient for you." Then in times of anxiety, even dread, or doubt or questioning, the baptized might find a settling peace in the victorious response of Luther, "I am baptized."

The second way to underscore the meaning of baptism is for the members of the congregation to re-present their own baptism during the act of baptizing. Re-presentation or reenacting is the biblical way of remembering. It is not enough to call forth in imagination an old memory. It is only enough or reenact one's own baptism in the context of the baptism now taking place within the liturgy. Two beautiful liturgical aids toward such reenactment are "The Baptismal Covenant" in *The Book of Common Prayer* of The Episcopal Church and "Reaffirmation of Baptism" in *The Lutheran Book of Worship*. The corporate nature of the reaffirmation of baptism should remind each individual of the supporting community about her or him as she or he runs the risks inherent in baptism, that is, participation in the death of Christ and the costs of discipleship. And the baptismal covenant revisited will be a reminder of the responsibility within community to nurture the newly baptized, whether adults or children; to care for the homeless, the hungry, and the alienated; and to increase the love of God and neighbor in the world. This completes the corporate nature of baptism, making it the "sociological sacrament," linking the church to society.[5] Perhaps the failure to see baptism as a sociological sacrament and thus to understand how it is related to the world beyond the church accounts in part for the failure to see the relation between faith and social ethics, which we shall look at in chapter 9.

The Eucharist

On a scale of one to ten, the Eucharist might occupy fifth place, behind caring people, prayer, human needs, and the Bible, in the forming of faith. About one-third of the professionals said the Eucharist ranged from important to very important in their faith formation. About half the laypeople placed it in that range. However, these figures tell less of a story with regard to the Eucharist than do figures relating to any other subject in our study. To illustrate, among the professionals the importance of the eucharistic event and its significance for faith ran the gamut from "absolutely unimportant" to the "hot spot" for faith, from "no different from any other meal, since every meal should be with the Lord" to the "center of the Christian experience—where the gospel is focused." In the latter vein one said, "It is as important to me as speaking in tongues is to a Pentecostal."

The Sacraments: What's Wrong?

For those professionals who maintained its crucial importance to faith, it was a means of grace, or an occasion of grace, as some preferred, through which Christ is received afresh. In and through it the Lord is experienced as really present. A pastor put it in incarnational language: "The Lord's Supper is rich with incarnation of God's ongoing grace, of his promise of the marriage banquet, of his involvement in the stuff of this world. In the Eucharist there is a re-presenting and a reexperiencing of God's incarnational love in Christ. Implicit in incarnation is forgiveness. With that background the Eucharist is the celebration of victory over sin and death. I experience this within a community of faith. Communion celebrates community through which my faith develops."

A few made the Eucharist purely symbolic, "an occasion for reflection and meditation that does not mediate grace," as a professor voiced it. He added that grace is mediated but through a sense of corporate identity, and the Lord's Supper is the occasion for that corporate mediation. Another saw the Lord's Supper as a "heightening of awareness that God loves us enough to give the best he had in order that his love would become believable." For those for whom the Eucharist was a fresh experience of grace, it became that either through the elements themselves, or as a symbolic reminder, or by way of the worshiping community. In the latter case the Eucharist seemed to provide a connectional or lateral dimension. It thus became a sacrament of grace and at the same time a sacrament of common humanity before God.

Before we turn to the laity in our sample, we ask what we are to make of the low assessment of the value of the sacraments in the forming of faith among the professionals. While the sixty interviewees were not representative of the more sacramental churches, they were from denominations whose traditions found baptism and especially the Lord's Supper necessary to faith. In fact, Calvin, a giant in the Reformed tradition, had defined the two marks of the church as the Word rightly preached and heard and the sacraments rightly observed. Since these were all professionals, and since they had formulated their theological positions rather carefully, it cannot be that they did not understand the sacraments or appreciate their historical or theological significance. The pastors especially, but also many professors, regularly were liturgists and/or preachers at services where the sacraments were observed. Their integrity would have required them to come to grips with what they were doing in an official capacity as well as within the purview of their own faith formation. These people simply did not appear to be comfortable without an understanding of what they were doing.

We have very few leads. But we do have the strong impression that while the sacraments did not nurture their faith in a very conscious way, they were present to them as some minor, some major, occasions along the faith journey. We surmise that they might have viewed them more as instruments, especially the Lord's Supper, for the nurturing of a congregation rather than for their own sustenance. One reason for this surmise is that the women and men in our sample did not seem to find in formal worship, such as baptismal and eucharistic services are, major occasions for the growing of *their* faith. They "conducted" such services, but their own growth, as far as they were consciously aware, came primarily in more intimate ways: a significant other or two, preparation for their professional duties (e.g., Bible study), the struggle for self-understanding, the quest for meaning, a continuing dialogue with God. A eucharistic service would raise consciousness, and might on occasion be a moment of grace; but seemingly it would not normally be a habitually chosen path to faith. We further observe that the paths they had chosen were simply different. Had they been of a more liturgical leaning, as their Episcopalian brothers and sisters, for example, the sacraments, especially the Eucharist, would probably have been much more up front in their faith formation. Profoundly, they saw what their own rich, unique pasts had prepared them to see. There are people to whom the sacraments appeal with great power, but most of our people were not among them. The sacramental possibilities were not compelling to them. Not that they were closed-minded—they decidedly were not. What was compelling to them came from a different orientation, and they looked with expectancy toward other fulfilling opportunities.

This simply takes seriously the uniqueness of each along the faith journey. Our pasts massively point us along the way. And while changes occur along the way to point us in relatively new directions, some possibilities beckon us and others do not. The faith journey is like any other journey: a basic direction served by many paths. No single map, not even one with a few clearly designated marks along the way, will suffice for all. The past of each is too orienting and the possibilities too numerous for all to be guided by the same means toward the ultimate goal. The lay experience is not basically different; that is, among the traditional means of grace, some means will be more efficacious than others. It does no good for faith to insist that what theoretically and even theologically would be expected to inform faith and nurture it, will and must. That would be the case of an abstraction foundering on the concrete reality of human experience.

The word "occasion" may suggest more precisely the value to which the church has pointed in its language, "means of grace." That language has tried to capture the notion that God is mediated through an event, for example, the Eucharist. But this suggests that God is outside of us and comes to us through, or by way of, an intermediary, such as the Lord's Supper. An occasion, on the other hand, as the word was sometimes used by people in our sample, is only possible at all because God contributes to that occasion's life, as God does to every happening. God is active in each and every occasion, participating in the baptism or in the Supper, for example, bringing persuasively to bear upon the occasion the divine vision for that moment that is coming to be. Every occasion has the possibility of being a revelatory moment. Nevertheless, occasions such as the Scripture reading and the eucharistic meal, because of sacred attributions made of them ("This do in remembrance of me") together with their unique histories, beget a set of expectations in participants that may yield a higher incidence of divine experience. We see what we are prepared to see, and we see God in some occasions more than in others. Our professionals found such occasions significant when those occasions enabled them and others to make finer responses to the God who had found them. Candidly, occasions other than the Lord's Supper may have better enabled some "eyes of faith" to focus on the ultimate Reality.

Half of the laity rated the Eucharist important to very important, but very few were able to say *how* the Lord's Supper is important to their faith. Fully one-third of the laity, on the other hand, characterized the Lord's Supper as not important for them or as perfunctory. Furthermore, about one-sixth of all the laity acknowledged that they had problems with Holy Communion; for example, it was not offered often enough; it was too scheduled, too planned, or too ritualized; it made one feel guilty or at least unworthy (i.e., one can't be angry and take Communion); its meaning was obscure and vague; it was too morose; it was too holy. So while half said the Eucharist was important to their faith, the other half tended to minimize its importance or lose some of its meaning in problems surrounding it. The laypeople did not offer much out of their experience about the Eucharist. But as we listened to them in the interviews and again on tape, we picked up a theological problem. Their expectations around the Lord's Supper, including a sense of guilt and unworthiness, and their vagueness as to how to think about it, suggests a lack of theological clarity. All knew Holy Communion had to do with the death of Jesus Christ, and all knew that that death was for their salvation. But for many the Lord's Supper had only a past tense to it, except as they were in the present facing backward toward the cross. Neither a freed, celebrative present, nor a beckoning future full of challenge, nor an eschatological future full of promise and hope, seemed to constitute the meaning of the Eucharist. Most people who did comment did so within an individualistic perspective. The sense of the human community being bound together in the Lord's Supper did not seem to be part of their theology either. A few might heartily assent to this statement of one of them: "It [Lord's Supper] is a reaffirmation of oneness even as it confirms our basic relation to God. It is a corporate act, overcoming our individualism. When all partake together I sense that there is order again. I feel a new dimension. There's hope again." Perhaps many more could have subscribed to this horizontal dimension of the Eucharist, had it been set forth to them, but there was no indication that it was part of their theological outlook. The Eucharist seemed to increase the individual's sense of aloneness despite the deep yearning for meeting. A table set for meeting became too often an isolating experience, thereby decreasing the individual instead of enhancing him or her in celebrative fellowship about the table.

Strangely, the theology of Holy Communion seemed trivial and vague. There appeared to be little theological depth to the table-event. This seems strange, given the Protestant history of the sacrament. In the Sixteenth Century, the century of the Reformation, the Eucharist was the major subject of disagreement among the Reformers. Its importance was highlighted in the debates over the theology of the Eucharist; for example, they debated *how* Christ was present in the bread and cup, whether the rite is *primarily* a memorial feast, and what the *effects* are upon worshipers. Despite their disagreements, the Reformers to a person held the Eucharist to be the climax of the liturgy, the gospel orally absorbed in the midst of Scripture, sermon, prayers, hymns. The six churches in our study in one way or another are part of the heritage of the Reformation, but the theology of the Lord's Supper seemingly has been eviscerated through the centuries. The Eucharist is a fairly common event—weekly, monthly, or quarterly—but it appears that the depth and breadth of the act's meaning has been lost in the ritual.

All is not lost, though. Mystery surrounds the Eucharist in the sense of a numinous experience, and loyalties are recommitted. But if theology is always in the service of worship, as William Temple claimed, and if clearer theology should enhance worship, then the narrow and limiting theological understanding of the Eucharist that most of the laypeople seemed to possess detracts from what the Eucharist might be for faith. At least the Lord's Supper seems to be more guilt producing than freeing. The guilt is not the "good guilt" one man talked about: "It's very powerful. You are sailing along in your self-sufficiency. The Lord's Supper says: 'Stop. Take a look.' It brings me up short. It doesn't discourage me, but it reminds me of my insufficiency. It makes me rework my orientation, my perspective on life." The guilt it seemed to produce for many was depressing: "I should be better, worthy of the bread and cup. I'm not," said one. And this guilt was not canceled by any lasting sense of good news. The head may have assented, but the heavy heart was loaded with a continuing sense of failure.

What we think our study has told us about Holy Communion is that there is an urgent need for theological table-talk, that is, talk about the Table and its several meanings in layered depths. A recovery of theological understanding by the layperson would seem to be crucial for this sacrament to be more fully efficacious in the development of faith. The World Council paper *Baptism, Eucharist and Ministry,* already referred to in the section on baptism, offers several topics for sermons as the pulpit points to the Table in the service of Holy Communion:

> The Eucharist as Thanksgiving to the Father
> The Eucharist as Anamnesis or Memorial of Christ
> The Eucharist as Invocation of the Spirit
> The Eucharist as Communion of the Faithful
> The Eucharist as Meal of the Kingdom[6]

Ten-minute meditations lifting up one point each Communion Sunday would give depth and breadth to the theology of the sacrament. There is such richness in each point in the World Council paper that repeating the five points in subsequent years would add depth to the breath of the theological vision. The act of partaking of the bread and cup begs for elucidation of its meaning so that the act clarified by understanding enables one to worship better. Worship in turn helps to shape faith.

Laypeople have a sense that Holy Communion is important to their faith, but they seem not to know why, in any theological depth. Educational opportunities in the classroom and from the pulpit might well redress the lacunae in the laity's theology of the Eucharist, as well as baptism. This would return people to their theological roots in the Reformation. Periodically, the old traditional "means of grace"—Bible, prayer, sacraments—need to be theologically revisited lest their values for faith become buried by mere repetition. Doing theology around the sacraments would not only make them theologically more alive but would also be a means of revisiting history to discover why the Reformers placed these sacraments at the center of the church's life. Though such knowledge guarantees nothing, it might help the church to accomplish its foremost task: bringing to birth and nurturing the life of faith.

NOTES

1. *In, Not of Living Our Baptism in the World* (Philadelphia: Lutheran Church Press, 1974). An excellent booklet in the LCA Adult Christian Education series.
2. *Baptism, Eucharist and Ministry,* Faith and Order Paper no. 111 (Geneva: World Council of Churches, 1982), p. 3.
3. As quoted by Philip S. Watson, *Let God Be God* (London: Epworth, 1947), p. 165.
4. *Baptism, Eucharist and Ministry,* p. 6.
5. Roland Bainton, *Here I Stand* (New York: Abingdon, 1950), p. 142.
6. *Baptism, Eucharist and Ministry,* pp.10-15.

CHAPTER · 8

The Sermon: An Impossible Task?

As we listened to 210 faithful people talk about Sunday mornings, we began to wonder more and more about the place of the sermon in their faith development. Since the pastors were on the giving end of the sermons, as were the professors from time to time, it may be understandable that they would have little to comment about, except around the stage of preparation, as they did when they talked about the Bible. But for 150 laypeople, whose faithfulness included a church service nearly every week, to virtually bypass the sermon when it was specifically asked about nudged our curiosity and pushed us to dig a bit. But not much was forthcoming.

Through the course of the interviews we came to understand some of the reticence. They seemed to be protecting their pastors. These were not only their current pastors. We had tried to get around their feelings about their present pastors by saying: "You've been in the church a long time. You've probably had several pastors, and you've heard a lot of pastors preach. We're not asking only about the preaching you are now hearing. Tell us about how you sense sermons have helped your faith." They still seemed hesitant to say much. When only a third could say that sermons probably helped them to grow, and even then could not be very specific, we had to wonder what was going on.

We learned a little. Soon after a pastor had begun his sermon (the sexist language is intentional, for references were to males), they pretty well knew where he would finally end up. His thought patterns were quite limited and predictable. The train of thought was carried on narrow-gauge rails and the listener got off at the first station. A few braver souls ventured to wonder out loud what preachers read, or if they read much at all. Perhaps the biases of the laypeople emerged here, for some wondered if their pastors were reading any classical literature, current novels and plays, or biographies and autobiographies. The question, gently raised, implied they thought sermonic content could benefit from wider reading. But it was also raised because some listeners thought the language of the preacher was trite and limited. Language patterns were part of the predictability of a sermon. It was easy to tune out language to which they had become so attuned. A few hardy ones spoke for others: the content was often platitudinous and the language trite. The result was soporific. But loyal laypeople hesitated to say this of previous or present pastors because they downright loved their pastors.

The vast majority of our laypeople expressed respect as well as affection for their pastors. They called attention again and again to their pastoral work, expressing gratitude to this pastor or that whose presence had been relieving and redemptive in crises in their lives. They respected them as people of God, clergy who actually manifested Deity to them. They were neither patronizing nor embellishing when they said their pastors were "fine human beings," "examples to the flock," "caring people," "people you'd like to have your children grow up to be like." So it was hard for them to be open and candid about their pastors' sermons.

Especially when the sermon is viewed in much of Protestantism as the single most important thing the pastor does, according to job descriptions of pastor nominating committees. They did not want to appear to be criticizing him.

A few wondered out loud how much preparation time the pastor spent on his sermon. The organization of the sermon was the question. It often seemed to them that the sermon rambled, as though the preacher was all over the map with little sense of destination. One wondered how such a preacher "ever knew when he was done."

No one in our sample accused the pastor of not preaching from the Bible. But some suggested that biblical preaching should open up the Bible rather than be a point of departure, opening it up for the congregation to behold as a rich piece of the whole tapestry. There seemed to be some yearning for the congregation to *participate* in the drama that is the Bible. This implied a criticism of preaching that does not really deal with the text and its context but uses a biblical verse or two in a superficial and prooftexting way. That is not the way they put it; but it is what we thought we heard some saying.

A final criticism of preaching was implied when some of the laity said that the sermon helped when it came from the preacher's heart. We heard two things: (1) a mere head trip was not helpful. When the sermon possessed the pastor, and when he preached out of a heart aflame with a passion that had ignited him, the communication gripped their feelings, too. (2) But mere enthusiasm on the part of the preacher was not it, either. There had to be some intellectual content to accompany, as well as be the base for, the passion of the pastor. Heart and head needed to come together in order to produce effective, helpful sermons.

In summary, what our lay sample told us was that

normally sermons were not very helpful in the forming of faith. Some divulged reasons: triteness of content and language, poor organization, limited biblical exposition, and a lack of balance between heart and head.

Is the Sermon an Impossible Task?

From neither pastors, professors, nor laity did we get much positive input to construct an answer to this question. We did get a few undeveloped clues. As we have presented some of the data from this study to church groups, including workshops with pastors, we have also gathered clues. And some of what follows is the result of our own reflection on the state of the sermon, quickened by the negatives in our sample and by the requirements that a theological vision places upon the unique communicative event called a sermon. We are making three proposals toward recovering the sermon—not for some former place it may have held, for those contexts are gone, but recovering it for a new role in eliciting feelings, beliefs, and commitments, for the enhancing of faith's vision of its Lord.

1. We begin with a statement from Karl Barth that raises a profound and disturbing question. "On Sunday morning when the bells ring to call the congregation and minister to church, there is in the air an *expectancy* that something great, crucial, and even momentous is to *happen*."[1] For Barth the expectancy is that God will be present. That is the happening! In the chapter on human needs we raised the question about the deep ontological need for the Ultimate and the Transcendent. Barth's statement locates that need reaching out in expectancy in Sunday morning worship. Worship is one context in which that need might be expected to be met, and the sermon should be a major catalyst providing a meeting between the worshiper and God.

Was Barth wrong about the expectancy? Do worshipers expect a happening? Perhaps, but if so, our people did not come out and say that in the words they spoke. Neither did the professionals. Yet perhaps that expectancy underlies why our laypeople trudged or motored faithfully to church on Sunday mornings. And perhaps it underlies why the preacher comes to the pulpit each Sunday morning. But neither preacher nor layperson talked about any "air of expectancy" nor about any happening. Nor did their words come close to such disclosure. Some talked about how much the people meant to them, some about the music, none about the liturgy itself, a few about the sermon (after we raised the question), but none about any happening where God would be present. Yet maybe that was the motivation, hidden even to themselves, drawing them to church on Sunday morning, as we suggested in discussing the need for ultimacy in chapter 2.

If so, the worship service itself, including "the Word rightly preached and heard," would seem to have incumbent upon it the responsibility of becoming the means by which "something great, crucial and even momentous is to happen." But our sample made little of liturgy and almost as little of the sermon. Perhaps the sermon is an impossible task in part because it has been made to bear too much of the Sunday morning load. Worship is often seen as preliminary to, or context for, the sermon. If God is present, there can be nothing that is preliminary or context, which is a form of reduction. The sermon may be looked upon historically and by the congregation as ideally the climactic act in worship, but its place is creaturely and limited. It is only one occasion among many in a worship service, for example, a hymn, or the Scripture read well, or the benediction as the final good word from God. All occasions can become a meeting between God and the worshiper, and the various parts of the worship service need to be seen as freighted with the possibility of being a meeting place between God and the soul.

In the chapter on prayer we suggested that some education is necessary to help the faithful broaden and deepen the prayer experience. Pastoral prayers should model for the congregation the steps of adoration, confession, thanksgiving, and supplication, and also model language as the vehicle of prayer. Prayers of the giants of church history, such as Augustine and Wesley, prayers from the Bible, upon which such giants depended, and the prayers of deeply spiritual contemporaries, such as John Baillie and Thomas Merton, are prayers that can serve as models in language as well as content. Prayers that beckon, lure, persuade, entreat, confess, convict, and supplicate are prayers that can take some of the load off the sermon, for they can help a worshiper have a momentary experience of leaning on the very balconies of heaven.

Music, to which some in our study paid high tribute in the forming of their faith, can also take the burden off the sermon. Some acknowledged that they had gained much of their theological knowledge through hymns. As we shall suggest later in this chapter, a mini-sermon now and then giving background for theologically appropriate hymns could further enhance that vital part of a worship service. Music connects powerfully with our primitive feelings. Perhaps it is the art form that lures the feelings of most people to greater depths and heights. Since feelings power us more than intellect, the more significant the role of music, the richer ought to be the entire liturgy.

The rest of the worship service, as response to the Presence, needs to be so designed and crafted, and so understood by the worshiper, clergy and laity alike, that during the hour some of the hundreds of bits of experiencing that are taking place between God and each

The Sermon: An Impossible Task?

in the company of the whole can be brought into conscious awareness. God is present to each in the total flow of that hour; such is the impact of Presence. If we could stop time, which we cannot, of course, every fraction of a second would bear the imprint of God on each soul. God is massively present with each breath we take to draw us beyond where we are to what we might become. Without God's creative and re-creative ministry all along the route of each life, including the hour of public worship, there would be bare nothingness. But that ministry of God to each is basically at the unconscious level. In the depths is the Spirit crying out with our spirits, "Abba, Father." Only now and again is this deep ministry of God to us brought to the surface, made conscious. Perhaps the primary role of worship is to help raise into conscious awareness what is always going on in the depths of our lives. Worship is not, therefore, a momentary break with the rest of our lives. It is in continuity with the rest of our lives. Its role is to lift up the eyes of faith to see a trifle more clearly what is always going on between ourselves and God. Worship is an hour of heightened sensitivity toward the God who is present. It is a primary and glorious moment when God gets our *attention*, even if sporadic, and that more focused attention reveals what God is doing, and what we should do, in all the rest of our living. Worship ought to enable us to listen for that Presence in the rest of our lives. Worship becomes a momentary vision of the Holy, helping us see what is constantly going on in the traffic patterns of our lives: within ourselves, before God, with others, in the midst of the creation.

2. Within worship the sermon is a special kind of communicative event. It is not a debate to win an argument, nor a political speech made to sway a crowd, nor an after-dinner talk made to provide a program, nor a lecture made to educate, nor a device to entertain.

Indeed, it is not a speech that fulfills human definitions of rhetoric. Perhaps this is where one of the problems lies: it may be compared to many kinds of speeches and found wanting. Then it is an impossible task.

The sermon is a Logos-event. The Logos, or Word, is God communicating to the creation, especially the human creation. The Logos, God's speaking to us human beings, creates us, judges us, redeems us. God is constantly trying to persuade us, gently for the most part, roughly at times, to be saved, that is, to be re-created in the divine image. For Christians the Logos became flesh, that is, became one with Jesus of Nazareth. The Word of God became incarnate, enfleshed. God's communication was fully appropriated by Jesus, and Jesus became the God-man. That union marked the eloquence of God, for in that "luminous moment" the Word of God fully shaped and formed a human being into the "spittin' image" of God. So that life, that death, that Resurrection are God's continuing communication to us: the Word in our midst, Immanuel.

The sermon is connected to that Word. It is a continuing communication of God to all who worship. The sermon consists of very human words, fully dependent upon the written Word, the Bible, pointing to the living Word, Jesus Christ, who is the quintessence of God's communicative achievement.

Some preachers deliver the sermon better than others, no doubt. Some are more gifted in linguistic skills, some in physical attractiveness, some in their personalities. If the sermon is a truly incarnate event and if God humbly uses whatever is available to speak the divine mind and intent, God must use what is offered. The offering might be poor, but God uses it nevertheless, enduring what was offered. Most preachers' offerings may be only average at best. But the point is that God uses what is available. The responsibility on the preacher is to make

The Sermon: An Impossible Task?

himself or herself as available as possible to God for the Word, the communication from God for that day, to come through. A preacher shows himself or herself to be a servant available to God by way of (1) careful biblical/theological research; (2) intentional listening for the Word to speak to him or her; (3) careful appraisal of the human condition through pastoral care, reading the world's literature (where God is also speaking), keeping abreast of the world's activities, and so on; and (4) careful crafting of the sermon itself.

Biblical research not only lets the Bible present itself more clearly; it might also help overcome lay biblical illiteracy. This evidently happened in the experience of a laywoman who said of her pastor, "By his preaching I came to a new understanding of the Bible; some of those stories were not what they seemed. His sermons were like a breath of fresh air."

Intentional listening would mean that the preacher hears God's message before he or she goes to the pulpit, and in that hearing some shaping of that disciple goes on. The message is first the preacher's, existentially. When God's Word has first taken hold of the person at the pulpit, it has a better chance of becoming an occasion of encounter between God and the person in the pew. As one of the laity said, "When the pastor is excited over what he is learning and imparts that to the congregation, then the sermon catches hold." Again Logos has become incarnate. The pew has witnessed it.

Careful appraisal of the human condition fulfills Barth's image of the preacher with the Bible in one hand and the newspaper in the other. The sermon must address the world of sin, tragedy, and death as well as the world of courage, aspiration, and love.

Careful crafting of the sermon will help pastors deal with the criticisms of poor organization and trite language. Human language at its freshest and best ought to be offered to God, as Jesus offered his fragile humanity, that God's awesome love might redeem the congregation that morning and send it on its way rejoicing.

The sermon, however, may still be an impossible task, at least for many preachers. They are administrators of budgets and programs, pastors in life's small and large crises, educators to some degree, conflict managers, and very often average in ability and skills. Furthermore, the sermon is not the only vehicle for God's communicative Word on a Sunday morning. In discussing our research findings with a committed and very intelligent adult church school class, we elicited some interesting suggestions. They wondered why there needed to be a "full length" sermon every Sunday. They seriously doubted if the average preacher could come up with forty-eight fairly good sermons a year. And was it realistic or fair to ask him or her to do so? Preachers whose sole or chief responsibility is the sermon may produce every Sunday. But they are an unfair measurement for the rest. They may be much more skillful in communication, and they have much more time for their specialty. Members of the class suggested that the average pastor in the average church should be expected to produce a superior sermon once a month, or to crowd those twelve into a specific time in the church year, such as Advent, Lent, or Pentecost. And the rest of the time? The class would feature music one Sunday a month with a five-minute meditation around one of the hymns or choral pieces, which themselves have grown out of Scripture. Through the centuries hymn writers, such as Bach, Mozart, Handel, and Beethoven, and musical interpreters have helped shape the church's theology as well as its vision. A meditation now and then based on one of their classical contributions might be a blessing for a congregation made drowsy by the average preaching.

An innovative suggestion was the use of guided imagery for another Sunday, in which the people, after a passage from Scripture had been briefly presented, are asked to close their eyes, imagine they are part of the scene pictured in the Scripture, and listen to what God might be wanting to say to them as they stand with Moses before the burning bush, or before Christ as he asks Peter if he loves him, or as they hear Amos condemning Israel "because you trample upon the poor" and charging them to "let justice roll down like waters." This would introduce the congregation to the possibilities in meditation that in the last thirty years have begun to make an impact in the United States. But guided imagery is a subject upon which the professionals and laity alike in our sample were almost totally silent.[2]

This church school class further proposed a teaching sermon (of twenty minutes?) on a passage of Scripture, out of which the pastor might or might not draw applications, but at least the passage could be opened up so that through it God might aim the congregation toward their own applications. This would be different from expository preaching as was suggested in our chapter on the Bible, since teaching *(didache)* is somewhat different from preaching *(kerygma)*, but it would be another effort to deal with biblical illiteracy. The class also saw no problem with a ten-minute mini-sermon once a month, with one point to be made crisply and clearly. And if the congregation is dismissed ten minutes early, the class felt that only a few compulsive people would complain, providing the one point was a good one, well made. They did not believe the congregation cared to hold a stopwatch on the preacher.

3. But the sermon, including the several meaningful alternatives, is still an impossible task if the congregation does not hear. The word "hear" is critical. It does not mean merely to listen to or at. The biblical way of hearing

is to hear obediently, to listen to and to answer, to give ear to and to act. A response is called forth. But to respond, one must have heard. This peculiar emphasis on hearing helps set the sermon, or its equivalent if that equivalent is based on the Bible, apart from most other forms of speech. Perhaps the sermon in one respect is closest to the theater, not as entertainment but as a form of communication that involves a response from the other. Søren Kierkegaard caught this point when he likened a typical church service to the theater: the preacher is the actor, the congregation is the audience passing judgment on the actor, and God is heaven-knows-where. Using the model of theater, Kierkegaard turned the whole thing around. The congregants are the actors; God is the audience, listening for the actors to speak their life-words; and the preacher is the prompter in the wings who "whispers the word to the listeners."[3] Concludes Kierkegaard, "If the speaker has the responsibility for what he whispers, then the listener has an equally great responsibility not to fall short in his task."[4] This makes Calvin's point that one of the marks of the church is the Word rightly *preached and heard*.

What the congregation brings to the sermon must be a willing heart: a heart set to obey not what the preacher says but what God might be saying through the Word preached. One laywoman said simply, "I enjoy sermons." That is what some people say as they go out the church door. But that's not it! Sermons are not for enjoyment, though that may be the coating for the medicine at the center. Another woman said, "When I come to church, I come to hear the Word of God and go home refreshed." That is not it either. Refreshed for what? Like the wise men who visited the infant Jesus, does she go home a different way? The worshipers, as they approach the church, bring with them deep questions, perhaps unconscious ones, as did the pastor as he or she worked on the sermon off and on all week. God meets those questions and provokes yet others by the answer that the Holy One *is, shares,* and *commands.* That answer, theologically stated, is redemptive love becoming incarnate in human hearts and transforming lives, and is meant to be spent to increase the love of God and neighbor in the world. The sermon is a *Meeting Place* of presences: God, who communicates the divine self to the cell of humanity gathered; the congregation, summoned by God to hear obediently what God has to say to them in that time and place; the preacher, already addressed by God in his or her faithful preparation, and now a Socratic midwife to help a new birth of commitment to take place.

But who has taught the congregation how to hear a sermon? That does not come naturally. Pastors would greatly benefit their own sermonic efforts and the laity if they would teach them what a sermon is and how to listen to it. The sermon is not merely a natural form of speech. It is the awesome communicative event that has for its model the Logos becoming flesh and the courageous response of faith of Jesus of Nazareth. The sermon is not the impossible task. It is more like the impossible possibility. God makes what is impossible possible. God is faithful. If the preacher and the people are also, what a meeting place!

NOTES

1. Karl Barth, *The Word of God and the Word of Man,* tr. by Douglas Horton (New York: Harper, 1957), p. 104.
2. A good resource for this would be Roberto Assagioli, *Psychosynthesis* (New York: Penguin, 1976).
3. Søren Kierkegaard, *Purity of Heart* (New York: Harper, 1938), p. 180.
4. Ibid., p. 181.

CHAPTER · 9

Faith Facing the World: The Ethical Dimension

In several areas we have noted striking differences between the professionals and thelaity; for example, there is a major emphasis on belief formation for the former, compared to a quite minor involvement for the latter. The ethical dimension is another area in which startling differences obtain. Only eleven of the professionals were silent about their ethical investment, while the other forty-nine made strong connections between their faith and their ethical commitments. About 78 percent of the laity admitted they had no particular involvement in social ethics, although they had deep concern about their own personal ethics. In this brief chapter we shall listen first to what the laypeople shared with us and second to what the professionals told us. Finally, we shall propose some reasons for the deep cleavage between these two groups.

The Laity

A breakdown of the 78 percent who did not see themselves as thinking much about social ethics or getting involved in social ethical action might be helpful, for they were not of one mind. About twenty people felt their responsibility to the world was to "spread the gospel and to testify." Another twenty-seven made no comments about global consciousness even when they were directly asked about it. Fifteen felt that social welfare efforts were spoiling the moral fabric of the country by breaking down self-reliance and responsibility, which they felt somehow diminished patriotism. The rest—about fifty-five—felt that faith should have a "horizontal component," as one called it; that is, faith should involve helping people, but they did not know how to implement that part of faith except with next-door neighbors or special giving such as at Christmastime. They admitted they did not reflect much about the implications of their faith for the world of need, largely because it was too confusing. They felt frustrated and powerless as individuals to do anything about major social problems. Some said, "We leave it to the church," evidently never noticing the contradiction. But a few agonized over their responsibility. As one man said, "I have not shed my guilt. How to share? There's where I feel guilty. If I'm selfish about what I have, I'm not living up to the purpose of God for me. I know God forgives, but I feel guilty nevertheless. There's a discrepancy in my faith which I can't resolve."

Only about 22 percent registered empathic concern about poverty, racial prejudice, war, crime, care for the aging, and conservation of natural resources (their listing). Yet while registering concern about these large social issues, most were doing very little by way of personal involvement, except as they might respond to specific needs when presented in concrete ways, usually in times of publicized crisis and most often with money. Much of this involvement centered around hunger. Nuclear war, arms control, conservation of natural resources, race relations, abortion, minority and female rights, housing, and so forth, if mentioned, were as quickly dropped. Such issues did not appear to be on faith's agenda.

While the area of social ethics was virtually neglected by most of the laity, personal ethics were of considerable concern. Well over half thought of themselves as dealing fairly and caringly with people and being sensitive to others' emotional needs, especially in the church, the neighborhood, and the work place. They visited the aging and the sick, worked with youth, and took meals to those nearby. But some were wrestling with guilt. One man said, "Business struggles tear the hell out of me inside. Treating people with feeling doesn't go in business, especially in sales. I have strong foundations in faith, but why am I compromising so much?"

The bottom line for most of the laypeople was this: trust in God and the divine order to make things right. Fifty-seven percent of the people said that. We did not understand the attitude in such a statement to be indifference to human suffering, nor complacency because God would make it right as only God could. Rather, we gathered that the people expressing such a sentiment felt themselves to be at a loss as to what they as individuals could do, except to give money.

The Professionals

One of the most striking parts of the interviews with the professionals had to do with their involvement in social issues. Forty-nine were heavily invested in poverty programs in Appalachia, agony over world hunger, ecological concerns, court suits against state governments, racial demonstrations, peace marches, fresh-air camps for slum kids, strike intervention, juvenile court projects, community mental health, work with black banks and credit unions, pre-school nurseries, work in migrant camps and in slums with people living on welfare and beset by crime, or mediation between civil rights leaders and city fathers. They were self-styled conservatives and self-styled liberals struggling to get uninvolved churches involved. They saw poverty rub out awareness, the victims living without hope. They saw others as hopelessly victimized yet living with indomitable hope. They were shocked at the subtleties of segregation. They were incensed by the trivialization of the churches and they exulted over the churches' heroic moments. They located a large part of their life agenda with people with horrendous needs. They saw this agenda shaping their reality and forming their faith. One said, "You cannot separate my faith formation from my political autobiography"; another, "My faith grew through the social crises"; a third, "Being made to come to grips with people and the issues helped shape me." Said a one-time fundamentalist, "I wanted to be where the Christian faith would meet its hardest test. If it worked there, I'd believe it." The forty-nine who talked of their ethical vision had a global consciousness that gave them a sense of world citizenship. A woman put it in personal terms: "If God is the God of the universe, then all is a part of God's concern, and I am to be vitally concerned with a world citizenship committed to justice meeting the needs of the world."

Faith commitment motivated passionate ethical concerns, but some found that social situations teased theology along. For these, ethical involvement outran their theology, so that theology was forever playing catch-up. God was seen to be active in the struggle in the streets. Their commitment shoved them into the streets. Later their theology tried to interpret what they were doing. An avowed socialist put it memorably: "The more I became a socialist, the more pious I understood myself." This person meant that political activity drove her back to biblical sources in a search for meditative material by which to be guided as she tried to express the ethic of love. She moved back and forth between biblical texts and political images and actions. She wrote prayers and shared them and so rediscovered the importance of the biblical tradition and language. She affirmed that this dialectic meant something for the development of her faith. "Not only did it develop me in a political sense, bringing me nearer to the left, it also brought me nearer to my own tradition or to the best strains of my tradition." What continued to bring her back to biblical/theological images—for example, the Exodus from Egyptian bondage—was the understanding from Christian faith that God is love. "Love is the meaning of life, and the only way to a meaningful life is to become involved in the stream of love. It means to feel yourself loved and to be very consequent, that is, to get into conflict with society as Jesus did, and die." Exodus, the cross, and Resurrection became powerful biblical symbols to inform the radical love ethic in which some of our people were deeply involved. The roots of this social sensitivity were sometimes in the subsoil of childhood and adolescence, sometimes in the seminary classroom, and sometimes in crushing contemporary events.

For the large majority, ethical sensitivity and activity were a reflex action of faith. If they believed in God, they must get into social action. God was the plaintiff against social injustice. Hurt and disappointed by what was going on in the streets, God would be in the streets, they reasoned. God's followers had to be there where the divine activity was going on. Theological convictions must lead to intervention in behalf of the poor, the depressed, the dehumanized. The Incarnation was paradigmatic not only for Christian theology but also for Christian ethics. Out of this paradigm most were motivated to take up the cross and plant it in the places of social injustice. As one stated it in the context of talking about the ethical life, "It means becoming drawn into his lifestyle, when you take up your cross." This group, empathic to the yearnings and cries of the dispossessed, was first empathic to a caring Presence in the world. Where these empathies met, the human spirit was agitated to make redress. Agitation gave way to action. They heard a Reality proclaiming social justice, and they tried to obey what they heard.

Numerous studies confirm the findings from our lay sample. Laypeople primarily focus on personal faith and enrichment rather than social concerns. Laypeople demand of the churches individual and family emphases, with social action programs dealing with racial justice, war and peace, hunger and poverty very low on any prioritized list. The higher priority of social ethical concerns among clergy as compared to laity is also a consistent finding in recent research.[1]

Why the Cleavage?

The information gathered in our study, only the essence of which is presented in these pages, clearly shows that the professionals had a much larger understanding of, and exercised a much larger role in, the area of Christian social ethics than did the laypeople. Both the understanding and the exercise related in a reflective way to their faith; that is, the professionals saw ethical involvement in a wide range of social problems as a necessary corollary of their faith. The laity, on the other hand, while relating their own personal morality to their faith, with few exceptions did not see their faith mandating them to combat social injustices and to right wrongs. Many pleaded ignorance and powerlessness.

We did not find that the difference between the professionals and the laity could be read in terms of liberalism and conservatism, for there were both types in both groups. Further it would be an oversimplification to brand as conservative one who did not get involved in social causes as it would be to label one a liberal who did. Psychological makeup would surely account some for the difference between those who get involved and those who do not. Some of our interviewees, both lay and professional, were passive, private, introspective (and perhaps introverted), and timid; others were active, private and public, introspective and extroverted, sometimes timid and sometimes daring. Following an indigenous bent, an individual might gravitate toward involvement in social issues or shy away from them.

Undoubtedly several factors conspire to keep the laity from relating their faith to the social problems that are all about them. Our society is marked by major differentiations. For example, religion becomes separate from politics, which encourages religion to leave the vast area of politics out of its agenda. That in turn supports the churches in limiting the role of religion to the individual and the family. Nationalism and patriotism become battlecries, and laity who do not know the Bible and its radical, all-inclusive ethic, acquiesce in making the political scene out of bounds for religion. So the question of war and peace is often not faced because of two domains, church and state, with the test of patriotism dominating in one domain, the status of one's soul before Christ in the other. Another factor is the fear that if a church gets involved in social action, or even discusses social justice issues, such involvement would likely be divisive. While there is evidence that this is not so, the fear encourages churches to stick to "the things of the Spirit."[2]

However, we think the cleavage between the laypeople and the professionals in our study, as far as the social/ethical dimension is concerned, has to do largely with whether one's theology informs one's ethical thinking and acting. We can find no difference between layperson and professional at the trust and commitment levels of faith. These are the salvation levels. On the basis of God's redemptive activity, God has laid a claim on all people. In trust and commitment the laity and professionals made their answers. They would trust and obey as best they could. But at the level of belief, which is faith seeking understanding, the difference is vast as we posited in chapter 1. We think the cleavage is due in large measure to the professionals' struggling with the meaning of faith and social concerns and to the laity's failure to do that struggling.

Glock and Stark make our point in this lengthy but valuable excerpt:

> Organized religion in the United States, we would assert, is currently much more on the receiving than on the contributing side of the value process. This is not because of lack of opportunity to make explicit what secular values should be, to elaborate on the implications of religious faith, or to question the existing normative structure. The avenues open to the church for making a contribution are many—sermons, church, periodicals, and educational materials, official pronouncements, church programs, discussion groups. The available audience is large; the majority of the population is regularly exposed to the church's influence through Sunday worship as well as in other ways. Yet, the evidence indicates that the church is not availing itself of its manifold opportunities. It is not, in fact, seeking to make explicit how men ought to behave, to what ends, and for what reasons.
>
> This is not to say that norms and values are ignored in what the church seeks to communicate. On the contrary, they are the major themes of much that is talked and written about. But the level of abstraction at which the topic is pursued has the consequence of leaving to other sources the final say in determining everyday norms and values. The church's emphasis is overwhelmingly on

man's relationship to God. The implications of the faith for man's relation to man are left largely to the individual to work out for himself, with God's help but without the help of the churches.

[For] the majority of Americans . . . the nature of a religiously inspired choice is not clear.[3]

What these authors are saying is that ethical values and social and ethical behavior are little informed by theological reflection. As they succinctly put it, "the nature of a religiously inspired choice is not clear."

What is the "nature of a religiously inspired choice"? We might turn to any number of eminent Christian ethicists, but we choose Reinhold Niebuhr. In his book *An Interpretation of Christian Ethics,* Niebuhr posits love as the ethical ideal always before us as requirement, but always eluding us as we reach out to love obediently. In our way is our sin; sin, that is, that is measured over against God the Creator, not against mere moral codes that degenerate into moralisms. The human being is finite, but that is not the central problem. Our evil wills have hold of us, and moral evil results. Sinful willfulness disobeys love. We avoid cynicism and despair—cynicism about whether any good can be done, and despair that throws up its hands in the gesture of hopelessness—only because there is a transcendent Love that forgives us, and out of gratitude and contrition we can start again. When life is viewed from this theological perspective, the perspective of transcendence, human beings can undertake social action with neither utopian expectations nor an air of self-righteousness.[4]

At least for the Christian, ethical decisions and actions require some understanding of these central doctrines elaborated by Niebuhr. If ethical behavior grows out of a faith that thinks about God and what God requires, that faith needs to be understood. "What does the Lord require?" Micah asked. "He has showed you, O man, what is good; and what does the Lord require of you but to do justice, and to love kindness, and to walk humbly with your God" (Mic. 6:8). This is theological reflection upon the ways of God with Israel: as God acts so must the people of God. God's requirements call for continuing theological thinking and acting. Such thinking informs ethical decision making and actions.

The professionals are in the business of doing such theological thinking, an implication of which would be a Christian social ethic. Laity are not schooled to do this kind of thinking; actually, the church does not encourage it except in relatively rare situations. Until the laity become at least somewhat competent to think theologically about the issues that confront them from near and far, we probably cannot hope for much understanding about troubling social ethics issues such as militarism, war and peace, capital punishment, poverty, and ethnic and racial prejudice. The churches will continue to be divided on such issues, partly out of biblical and theological ignorance. We can cross-reference this point with the need for a deeper understanding of prayer, for a different level of Bible study within support groups, for at least a partial recovery of the sermon, for a new vision of the sacraments as connecting with all the rest of life. The sermon, prayer, the Bible, the sacraments—these when profoundly understood and meaningfully participated in have radical implications for Christian social ethics. As Glock and Stark pointed out, "The avenues open to the church for making a contribution are many . . . the available audience is large." But how we ought to behave, to what ends, and for what reasons, the churches fail to teach by not helping the laity to become competent theologians. Theologically illiterate may be too strong a description of the laity. But if the 150 laypeople in our study are among the most faithful in their churches, and if they are representative of faithful people everywhere, what about the not-so-faithful? And what about the social ills, how will they be healed? As faith faces the world, can it understand that world theologically and act with renewed commitment, trusting Grace for forgiveness of failures along the way? Again, the answer would seem to put a heavy burden on the church as educator. And the one person in most churches who is professionally trained to be a theological educator is the pastor. As the rabbi, or teacher, in the congregation, is he or she theologically skilled and able through good educational processes to help the laity become competent theologians, so that they can learn to view the human situation from the perspective of the Eternal? First-class continuing education events for clergy and sabbatical leaves (monitored by appropriate judicatories) could be important ways to enhance the training of the parish clergy for their crucial role as rabbis in the congregation.

We are not minimizing the problems inherent in teaching the laity to do theology for its own sake, in order to worship God more deeply, and in order to follow God's leading into the world of broken relationships and social injustice. Some personalities do favor left-brain, logical discourse; others right-brain, emotional discharge. Whether from an early inhibition of childhood's sense of wonder and curiosity, or from the fear of taking risks, or from poor modeling by important people for whom reading and thinking were a waste of time, or from mental laziness, many people do not really want to think. The old saw that 2 percent of the people think, 8 percent of the people think they think, and 90 percent of the people would rather die than think has enough truth in it to constitute the humor. Yet in the lay part of our study there did seem to be a yearning on the part of some to learn how to think theologically so that they could become theologians in their own right. If they could have that yearning fulfilled, they should be able to address their responsibility to deal with complex social problems clamoring for resolution, especially since ethics is a fundamental part of theology, owing motivation and direction to some systematic thought about God and God's ways with the world.

The question arises, What will quicken and inspire the eros within each to want to think theologically about ethical situations? The mind does need to be eroticized. The ultimate biblical commandment is to love God and neighbor, and the love of God includes loving with the mind. The function of the rabbi in the congregation, whether that teacher is ordained or not, is to so stimulate others that they develop a love affair with theological ideas and try to see how they fit the world in which they live. That world is the setting for the consideration of ethics.

NOTES

1. Cf. Dieter T. Hessel, *Rethinking Social Ministry* (New York: U.P. Program Agency, 1980), pp. 48ff.
2. Cf. ibid.
3. Charles Y. Glock and Rodney Stark, *Religion and Society in Tension* (Chicago: Rand McNally, 1965), pp. 182, 183.
4. Cf. Reinhold Niebuhr, *An Interpretation of Christian Ethics* (New York: Harper, 1935), *passim*, esp. chaps. 1–4, 7, 8.

CHAPTER · 10

Some Final Gleanings

In this closing chapter we bring together a proposal, a finding, and a vision. The proposal is that congregations incorporate a research component into their programming. The finding is that faith is far more evolutionary than revolutionary in its formation, which would further emphasize the place of caring people within a congregation. The vision is the vision of God that emerged as faithful people talked about the One in whom their faith was deposited.

The Proposal

Not one of the 210 people knew of any empirical research in congregations about which they were knowledgeable. This would include research on any topic: giving or stewardship, evangelism, faith formation, human needs, educational levels, theological or biblical literacy, adequacy of caring, worship evaluation, and so on. By research we do not mean a professionally engineered project or a large-scale statistical analysis. We have something much more modest in mind. A pastor, especially with the help of a small committee composed of a businessperson or two, an educator, and a full-time homemaker, can design a small project to find

Some Final Gleanings

out answers to any number of questions that are facing or should face a congregation.

The gospel itself raises many theological questions and gives its own unique answers. For example, the biblical understanding of sin is not a research question in the sense of empirical research. But how a congregation thinks of sin, whether in a biblical sense, a moralistic sense, as a human failure, and so on, would be very informative to one preparing a series of sermons on sin, or to a church school class in theology. In the chapter on human needs we lifted up six needs our research uncovered. Would a simply designed project to ferret out needs in any congregation support or deny or add to our list? But far more important: how can ministry within a congregation be conceived and carefully implemented unless those responsible for that ministry know what human needs that ministry should try to meet? Or again: does any given congregation hold in fairly low esteem the two Protestant sacraments, as the 210 faithful people of our study did? If so, what do congregants say might turn that appraisal around?

These three research topics are suggestive of a large number of possibilities for research in a congregation. At the risk of seeming crass, we are wondering if a market analogy might be fruitful for congregations. Most businesses, small and large, do market analyses, by which they hope to discover the needs within their markets, the products that offer some promise of filling those needs, and the best way to package and market those products. The analogy ends there. But congregations might do their special business better if they were to gather from the members some information about what they think the church should do for them, as do secular businesses, even if this way of putting the question misunderstands the church. Only when misunderstandings are reckoned with can they be corrected.

Research methods can be relatively simple. Questionnaires are rarely simple and require some sophistication generally, including some pretesting. But they can be helpful. So can interviews of fifteen or twenty people randomly selected from a congregation of two hundred, if the interviews are conducted with some sensitivity and skill. Confidentiality is required, of course. Some questions can be asked, such as "How have three people been helpful to your faith formation?" Or getting various church groups to talk about the meaning of baptism *for them* could provide valuable insights to a pastor who wants to make that sacrament more meaningful to the congregation. Nearby colleges and universities probably have teaching staff skilled in research, some of whom could be employed for a reasonable honorarium to help construct an instrument and evaluate it for research within a congregation.

This proposal for research would help to develop a cutting edge within a congregation, by letting the laity tell how it is with them and by suggesting to the laity how seriously the church leadership wants to deal with them where they are in their faith pilgrimage. The gospel has its thrust toward the people of God. Empirical research can indicate the needs, wants (real and spurious), and stuckness or ruttedness of the people of God. Then ministry might be redesigned to help effect the work of the gospel in the lives of the people. That should make for a more vital congregation in witness and service.

The Finding: Evolution Versus Revolution

As we noted in the Introduction, about 90 percent of our total sample came to their faith through an evolutionary process, that is, through gradual growth, while about 10 percent had a revolutionary or dramatic faith experience producing marked inward change, according to their testimony. The primary means for faith formation, whether the route was evolutionary or revolutionary, was the same: caring people, as we have already noted. The preponderance of those whose faith formation was by way of gradual growth (with dramatic moments now and then to be sure) underscores the role of those who in their quality of caring could at times "run and not be weary," but most of the time could "walk and not faint" (Isa. 40:31). Said in different words and in different ways, many of our interviewees were almost a chorus reiterating the famous thesis of Horace Bushnell, "That a child is to grow up a Christian, and never know himself as being otherwise."[1] One said it symbolically for the many: "Maybe, like Timothy, my faith began in my mother's womb." There seemed to be an environment of caring people, whether in childhood, adolescence, or adulthood (often all three), midwifing the birth and continuing the nurture of faith.

Toward the close of chapter 3, two suggestions were made that could help churches educate and encourage their people to become more caring: (1) give to them, and ask from them, a deep sense of responsibility, and (2) accentuate the essence of the gospel, namely, that each is acceptable as he or she is before the Lord. Beyond the requirements of being responsible and accepting the fact that they are accepted by God's grace, caring people need to learn *how* to love. Love does not come naturally. The art and skill of loving, which finds its way out of the self into the caring attitudes and behaviors so essential to faith formation whether evolutionary or revolutionary, must be cultivated. Love is not one of Plato's or Aristotle's four cardinal virtues. It is one of Paul's three theological virtues: faith, hope, love. The kind of love Paul had imaged before him as he looked at Christ was first a grace-gift, then a command to love after the manner of Christ, and finally an act of obedient response in which the will is front and center. H. Richard Niebuhr has defined the goal of the church as the "increase among men of the love of God and neighbor."[2] Niebuhr then went on to say what this love means: "rejoicing in the presence of the beloved, gratitude, reverence and loyalty toward him."[3] This kind of love—the *agape* form—must be taught for what it is, a grace-gift from God; then it must be nurtured into a skill and an art to be shared. It may be one of the cruelest impositions imaginable to repetitiously thrust upon a congregation the commandment to love, with all the guilt that can create, without helping a congregation to learn how to love. If a psychiatrist has felt the need to write a book on the art of loving, calling it an inquiry into the nature of love, how much more should church leadership work on helping a congregation to learn the art of loving. The loving it would be talking about primarily would be the "more excellent way," that is, the wise and careful expression of the finest of God's grace-gifts.[4]

If one were to enter the demurrer that one has to be realistic, that a great many people may not be able to be taught the skill and art of loving, there can only be agreement. Some people may be too deeply wounded by life's onslaughts to feel they can afford to love, although "wounded healers" may make the very best lovers, as Henri Nouwen has shown. But the burden here is not to grasp for the moon. A few deeply caring people, sometimes just one or two, were enough for our sample. If the churches were to grasp and use the Remnant concept of Israel within Israel,[5] as identified in the magnificent Servant Songs of Isaiah 42–53 by the unknown prophet of the Exile, perhaps they could leaven the whole lump while they helped to create a milieu of caring, so that faith would be caught by young and older alike, whether gradually over the years or in a peak-experience, and that faith might command a person's entire lifetime.

The Vision of God

Since the essential question of this study is *how* faith is formed, the actual content of that faith was not up front. Consequently, the interviewees did not delineate their concepts of God although by statement and by implication a large number gave us glimpses into their vision of God. We are using vision to indicate what the eye of faith beholds as the soul is trained on God.

At the center of their vision of God many of these faithful people held to a notion of *power* that was not traditional. They did not minimize divine power, but they seemed to envisage it as the effective power of love among myriad effective powers. There was no reducing of divine power to its being merely first in a series of hierarchical powers. God was seen as Creator, as no other power was creator. But God in the divine creative power was not seen as hammering, forcing, coercing, imposing. Several of our subjects eschewed the use of the phrase "will of God," not because they believed God has no will or is ineffective, but because they had gradually come to a different sense of the divine will that could not be encapsulated in older connotations of that term. There was much expression of power as grace, not sheer will. We are not suggesting that this contrast is particularly new. What appears to be novel is the degree to which a different interpretation of divine power had become a near total perspective with them. God was not sole Creator; therefore, they owned responsibility for their own creativity in responding to God's pressure upon them. Yet God was Creator working to effect the purposes of the Divine in their lives and all creation. They were very conscious of laboring with a divine Ally whose love constantly pressured them from the region of immanence to respond to the needs of their world as God had responded to them. A clergywoman made the point this way: "I see God much more as the undergirder and sustainer, whom you might call a mother-figure, than as the authoritarian lawgiver or patriarchal figure. No longer do I feel that it is essential to talk in terms of submission to God's will as being the essence of theology, as if God were a kind of dictator who was interested in having others submit to a certain pre-patterned will he had for them. I now understand God more dynamically in terms of the creative power God uses in interaction with all of us to accomplish the work he is doing in the world."

Another way in which their perception of God's power was significantly different from the traditional one was God's role as lawgiver and judge. They saw God as moral power; that is, at the most elemental level there is a Goodness, a Presence, whose sole aim is to bring about goodness in the universe. But they did not see that Presence as tyrannical. God is not the extension of a churlish, impetuous parent. God is not an eye in the sky watching for signs of misbehavior. For very few of our sample did God come off as moralistic or legalistic, concerning whose touchiness one had to be on one's guard lest one offend. Even for those who expressed God's power in more traditional language, that power did not appear to be imprisoning or moralistically intimidating. This perception came late for many, both clergy and laity, sometimes after therapy had clarified God from a parent, sometimes after a deepening religious experience in their thirties and forties. One found a surrogate father "who gave me a new insight into that aspect of God's character that makes him Father and Friend, instead of that cold sort of God whose image is that of Judge, and a rigid image it is."

A favorite image of God as liberator emerged among both professionals and laity. This image was not in place of Savior. It had more to do with God's guiding, directing, leading, and freeing. It did not seem necessarily to connect with any liberation theology, although it may have come out of association with liberation movements, for example, those of blacks and women. It was not formalized into a system, at least as people talked with us about God as liberator, except by two people, both professors. The center of this image was on the one who frees the human being. The experiences that lay back of the image appeared to have a lot of serendipity in them, as though there were acts of grace occurring within the crunch of life and leading to an unplanned and unexpected outcome. One put the experience in these words: "Heh, that was an act of grace. There was God redeeming. That is what he is like. God is full of good surprises." Another characterized the divine serendipity: "Because of God, life is a whole series of new beginnings."

One outcome of seeing God as liberator was that almost all 210 people felt relatively free. It was as though, with a fairly strong sense of freedom—a gift of God—they had come to know themselves as responsible and had enjoyed their responsibility with all of the freight it carried. Though they confessed missing the mark more often than they hit it, they experienced their freedom as adults with little sense of nagging guilt and with a willed intentionality to try to do the will of God within the concretions of minute by minute existence. They came off as strong people who confessed that whatever strength they had came mainly from God, who had freed them to grow and to labor in God's liberating ministry in the world.

It might be expected that this vision of God, briefly described, emerged from what they had seen and heard in Jesus Christ. As a matter of fact, explicit reference to Jesus was infrequent. And the few who made explicit reference did so sparingly. We would have thought that when considering the question of faith formation, they would have focused with some degree of intensity on Jesus Christ. There were a few rich moments of talk about Jesus. For example, one said, "Over all is the heroic figure, Jesus, who has captured my allegiance and loyalty. Without that exposure I don't think I would have understood the meaning of my own life. The heroic dimensions of the life of Jesus Christ made me want to be a hero someplace." Another put it philosophically: "Jesus was a kind of concretion of the authoritative moral purpose in the universe which gives significance to life."

While we have very few of these statements, throughout the interviews ran the controlling notion of incarnation, with its corollary of immanence. A large number put incarnation in terms of God's risking; that is, that God is in the midst of the human muddle taking risks, paying the high price of those risks, struggling to achieve victory, and liberating through the Deity's struggling and paying the price. Love, in the expensive way of incarnation and cross, together with a confident hope expressed in Resurrection language, seemed to point to a luminous figure infrequently mentioned but massively present. Why there was so little explicit christological talk among both professionals and laity we do not know.

But God loomed very large! And the vision they had of God remarkably resembled that gentle, loving, risking, suffering, and victorious person, Jesus Christ, even though he was rarely named. There was a foreground figure giving the vision its form, content, and clarity; helping to focus the eyes of faith on the One whose glory he was revealing; and sustaining faith on its long and exciting journey. Along that journey the eyes of faith had seen a compelling vision, and they were eager to see more.

NOTES

1. Horace Bushnell, *Christian Nurture* (New Haven: Yale, 1947), p. 4.
2. H. Richard Niebuhr, *The Purpose of the Church and Its Ministry* (New York: Harper, 1956), p. 31.
3. Ibid., p. 35.
4. Erich Fromm, *The Art of Loving* (New York: Harper, 1956).
5. Cf. Gordon E. Jackson, *Pastoral Care and Process Theology* (Washington, D.C.: University Press of America, 1981), pp. 232-37.